Gift FROM THE River

AND OTHER STORIES

Loron Wade

REVIEW AND HERALD® PUBLISHING ASSOCIATION

Since 1861 | www.reviewandherald.com

Published by Review and Herald® Publishing Association, Hagerstown, MD 21741-1119

Review and Herald® titles may be purchased in bulk for educational, business, fund-raising, or sales promotional use. For information, e-mail SpecialMarkets@reviewandherald.com.

The Review and Herald® Publishing Association publishes biblically based materials for spiritual, physical, and mental growth and Christian discipleship.

Unless otherwise indicated, Bible texts in this book are from the King James Version.

Scripture quotations marked NASB are from the *New American Standard Bible,* copyright © 1960, 1962, 1963, 1968, 1971, 1972, 1973, 1975, 1977, 1995 by The Lockman Foundation. Used by permission.

Texts credited to NIV are from the *Holy Bible, New International Version.* Copyright © 1973, 1978, 1984, 2011 by Biblica, Inc. Used by permission. All rights reserved worldwide.

Texts credited to NKJV are from the New King James Version. Copyright © 1979, 1980, 1982 by Thomas Nelson, Inc. Used by permission. All rights reserved.

This book was
Edited by Kalie Kelch
Copyedited by Vesna Mirkovich
Cover designed by Daniel Anez / Review and Herald® Design Center
Interior designed by Emily Ford / Review and Herald® Design Center
Typeset: 11/13 Minion Pro

PRINTED IN U.S.A.

17 16 15 14 13   5 4 3 2 1

Library of Congress Cataloging-in-Publication Data

Wade, Loron, 1938-   .
  Gift from the river and other stories / Loron Wade.
     pages cm
  1. Christian converts—Biography. 2. Conversion—Christianity. I. Wade, Loron, 1938- Gift from the river. II. Title.
  BV4930.W33 2012
  242—dc23

                              2012040042

ISBN 978-0-8280-2696-3

Dedication

To Ruth Ann,

wonderful friend and faithful companion,
with deep gratitude for 50 years—and counting.

Contents

The Transforming Power of His Love

You know, Jesus did some surprising things. Sometimes He rebuked people who were expecting to be praised. But more often He showed compassion to individuals who never thought they could possibly be loved.

The stories in this book are about surprises like that. They deal with folks who were running along on the track of life, unaware that God had set a switch that would send them off in a totally different direction. That kind of change is, in fact, pretty close to the Bible definition of *conversion*.

As you read these accounts, you will be impressed by the vastly different ways in which His love reaches people of different cultures, ages, and languages, and the wide range of responses people have to God. Some He just sort of taps on the shoulder, and they step lightly into the path of salvation; for others it is not so easy, and the Lord has to wrestle them down to the mat.

When love comes in, everything changes; and when it takes over, the results are amazing. In fact, that word *amazing* shows up a lot in these pages because people whose lives God has touched tend to say they are "amazed" at what happened to them, meaning it was unexpected and they have no way of explaining it.

More than mere stories, these are testimonies that witness to the transforming power of His love. As Pat Grant says eloquently:

"I stand in awe, unable to speak
    that a Man who has power would be so gentle and meek
    and condescend to me
    so that I might see
    that the life I was living
    was never meant to be."

Chapter 1

A Gift From the River

. . . .

Doneshor Tripura

It seemed like an ordinary day, such a completely common and ordinary day that I never imagined it would end up being the most memorable day of my life.

The weather was warm, but that is what we expect in May in the southeastern part of Bangladesh, where I live. I was herding my father's seven water buffalo, but there was nothing unusual about that, either. In fact, I had taken care of these animals many times since early childhood, although in recent years I had done it less because I was finishing high school in our home village of Kumardonpara. But recently I had successfully sat for the final examination, so that day I was happy and relaxed, enjoying the natural beauty of the area in the company of a friend.

The broad waters of the Chengi River flow by my father's pastureland. About noon, when the heat seemed especially strong, I decided to slip in for a cooling dip. Because it was the dry season, the river was not very deep, so I jumped down from the bank and started walking through the water toward the center of the river, intending to find a deeper spot.

As I made my way out into the river, something caught my eye. Far upstream I could see an object floating down the river. I am not sure why this caught my attention, because there is certainly nothing unusual about that. But for some reason I stopped where I was and waited. I was happy to see that the current was bringing the object directly to where I was standing.

When it had come close enough, I was surprised to see that it was a book floating half submerged in the water. I could see its blue cover and red edges. When the book had come almost to my feet, my eyes opened in amazement as I read the words on the cover: *Pobitro Bibel.*

"Look!" I called to my friend, who was watching from the bank of the river. "It says 'Holy Bible.'"

In my home we were devoted followers of the Hindu religion and its gods, especially Radha and Krishna. Every morning and evening our family gathered to pray and place an offering on their altar, and we never failed to fast twice a month and observe Durga Puja each year, bringing the required offerings and animal sacrifices to the temple.

I had heard of the sacred book of the Christians, but I had never seen one. In fact, I had never felt any curiosity or desire to look at a Bible or know anything about it. But our parents had sown in our hearts a deep reverence for holy things, so when I saw the title of this book, I thought, *If this is a holy book, what is it doing in the water? I will take it out and treat it with respect.* So I picked up the Bible and got out of the river to look for a place I could lay it with its pages open so the sun could dry it out.

That evening when it was time to return home, I saw that the holy book was still quite damp, so I took it home and, without saying anything to my father, put it in a safe place. For the next three days I took care of the Bible, carrying it with me every day to the country and placing it in the sun and turning its pages so that they could dry completely.

By the end of the third day I saw that the Bible was dry. Then I began reading it. First I read about the Creator God who made everything in heaven and earth. From childhood I had read the Hindu scripture, especially the Gita, but I had never heard of the concept of a Creator of the world.

I continued to read and soon came to where it speaks of the creation of Adam and Eve. The Gita also says that the first human beings were a husband and wife, called Manu and Shatarupa. I thought that this must refer to the same individuals under a different name. Then I read that the woman was created from a part of the man and that when he saw her, he joyfully said, "This is bone of my bones, and flesh of my flesh!" This was a new and surprising idea to me.

After that I read about how sin entered the world and wickedness laid hold of humanity. As the days passed, I continued to study the Bible. One unforgettable day I read in Matthew 6:9-13 the prayer that Jesus taught His disciples, and I thought, *Up to now, all my prayers have been selfish. I have done nothing but ask and ask, wanting to get a benefit for myself and my family. Now I understand that the Christian concept of prayer is broad; it embraces the world.*

As I continued to read, I discovered the picture of a God who comes to people and invites them to accept His beautiful gift of salvation. He is patient, and He loves to forgive. All my life I had been trying to earn the favor of the gods by giving them expensive gifts and by doing tiring works of appeasement. The rich people I knew could easily win approval, but it was difficult for a poor family like ours to ever please the gods, because they always wanted more and more.

I soon realized that I was studying the Gita more than in all my previous years because I felt a fervent desire to compare it with the Bible and discover the truth. Finally I decided to take a red pencil and mark everything I found to be good and helpful in the Bible and to do the same with the Gita. But I soon gave up on this idea because in the Gita I could find something to mark only once in a while, whereas if I wanted to mark everything good and helpful in the Bible, I would end up marking the entire book.

The day I came to this conclusion I made two decisions: I decided not to read the Gita anymore. I also understood that I would one day become a Christian, although I had no idea when it would happen. I had been studying and comparing the two books for a year, and in all that time I had never met a Christian with whom I could talk about the things that were on my heart.

About this time I left home to study at Raojan College, in the city of Chittagong. As the pressure of my studies and other activities increased, I dedicated less and less time to spiritual searching. Five years passed rapidly, and at the end of this time I graduated and returned to my father's house.

I was attending to family responsibilities one day when I went to the public market in Khagrachari, a city about four miles from our village. There I met a friend from high school. After greeting him, I asked, "What are you doing now?"

"I work for a Christian church," he told me.

When I heard these words, a great joy filled my heart. "You are a Christian?" I asked him.

"Yes," he said, "I am a Seventh-day Adventist Christian."

"Come! Come!" I said, and I took him to a place we could talk. As soon as we were away from the noisy market, I told him about the Bible that had come to me on the river, and then I asked him the question that had been in my heart for so long: "How can I be a Christian?"

When my friend heard my question, his face showed a great happiness, and he gave me a strong hug. Then he told me that in Diginala, about 14 miles (22 kilometers) from Khagrachari, there was a house of worship where I could receive instruction about these things, and he invited me to attend.

The next Saturday I went to Diginala and found the house my friend had told me about. When I got there, the people were all sitting quietly with their eyes closed. I did not know that they were praying. I entered and sat down next to my friend, but I did not close my eyes. Instead, I looked around to see who was there. I liked what I saw. It appeared to me that these were normal people. When they opened their eyes, everyone was astonished to see me, and my friend was very happy.

After that, I began to attend the church in Diginala, although I could not go every week, because the bus fare cost 35 takas (about US$0.50), and I often didn't have enough money.

But there was great joy in my heart, and I began to talk to my friends in Kumardonpara about what I was learning. Some of them wanted to go to Diginala too, so we agreed to take turns, and two or three of us would go every Sabbath with the money we could get together. Then the ones who had gone would return and teach the others what they had learned.

For a year we attended this way. Then I told the pastor, Ruram Orbit, that I wanted to be baptized because I felt a great desire to formally belong to the church. He made the arrangements for Pastor Dilip Hagidok, secretary of the East Bangladesh Region, with its offices in Chittagong, to come for the baptism.

The little chapel in Diginala didn't have a baptistry, so they told us the baptism would take place in the Chengi River. When I heard this, tears filled my eyes because I realized that in the same river that had brought me the Bible I would be sealing my covenant with God.

On November 13, 2002, 25 people were immersed in the clear waters. I and seven of the friends I had invited were among that number. We are the firstfruits, the very first Christians among the Tripura people.

I asked the pastor how I could learn more about the Bible so I could teach as many people as possible. He told me about the Bangladesh Adventist Seminary and College and made arrangements for me to attend.

In the first summer vacation I joined with the seven friends from my village who had been baptized with me to build a simple bamboo structure that was the first Christian chapel in all that area. After graduation I began to work for a nongovernmental aid agency in Khagrachari. My friends are leaders in the local church, which continues to grow.

* * * *

Perhaps I should add a curious note: About a week after I received the Bible from the river, I was working at the house of one of my friends, and I heard him say angrily to his father, "Where is my Bible? Did you do something with it?"

"Yes," his father said, "I threw it into the river. If you keep reading that book, you will become a Christian, and here we are all Hindus."

When I had a chance to speak to my friend, I told him about the Bible that had come to me on the water.

"Yes," he said, "that is my Bible." And he told me that he had received it as a prize for completing a correspondence course offered by the Baptist Church.

"Well, I have it now," I told him.

"That's all right," he said. "You keep it. I am not interested in it anymore."

And I am sorry to say that to this day he has not shown any more interest in studying the Bible.

Chapter 2

A Good Conversation

. . . .

Mario Veloso

In a city where I was serving as a pastor in Argentina, a young priest was just beginning his ministry. Because of one of those circumstances of life that can happen to anyone (it could have happened to me), he became entangled in a romance with the daughter of an important merchant of the city. The matter was discovered, and the father of the young woman was, shall we say, more than a little indignant. Even though the matter had to do with his own daughter, he felt so betrayed, so shattered, by what had happened that he took it upon himself to go to the newspaper. Soon the affair made headlines in the whole city. As a result the very foundations of the young priest's world were shaken, and he, of course, had to leave.

The day he left, a tremendous rainstorm dumped torrents of water over the whole region. And on that same day I had to travel to another of the cities in my far-flung pastoral district. There were no paved roads in those days, and the rain made the highways impassable, leaving only one mode of transportation: the train, which went through the area once a day.

I went to the station, bought my ticket, and got on. The right side of the car was nearly full, but for some reason only a few people were sitting on the left, most of them down toward the far end. But there, about halfway down, the young priest was sitting by himself. I recognized him, of course. Who in that town wouldn't have? His picture had been on the front pages.

I went straight to where he was and sat down. I didn't say a word, and neither did he. The passengers continued to get on until, pretty soon, it was time to leave, and the train began to move along the tracks with all the jerks and clacks that are typical of trains everywhere.

"How are you?"

When he looked at me hesitantly, I added, "Don't answer. I know how you must feel. I would feel the same."

"You know?" he asked.

"I'm sorry," I answered, "but who wouldn't?"

He shrugged. "You're right, of course. I feel terrible."

"You know something? God doesn't reject you. Maybe people will for a while, but not God."

"What do you know about God?"

"Not much," I replied, and we began to talk.

I dealt with him the way I would have dealt with a pastor from my own church had the same thing happened to him. Little by little he began to open his heart. We talked as if we had been friends forever. At times he wept like a child. He was suffering as any human being would under those circumstances. We traveled for five hours, talking the whole way. When I got off the train, we embraced, and I said to him: "Remember, the Lord forgives!"

"Yes," he said, "I know that, and now I know it better than before. I hope we can meet again. Your conversation today has been very good for me."

"If the Lord wills, we will meet again," I said, "and if not, remember this book. It will help you all your life." And I gave him a book that talks about how to center our lives in God's love.

After another embrace and farewell, I got off. As the train pulled out of the station, I stood on the platform, and he stood at the window waving goodbye.

It was, of course, highly unlikely that we should ever meet again because he was on one pathway in life and I on another very different one. So it was not realistic to expect that our paths would cross again. That is why I worked with him for those five hours as if all eternity depended on that conversation.

Sometime later I was visiting in the northern part of my district, where there was an Italian community. You know, Italians are wonderful people. How I love them! They are so spontaneous and filled with energy and vitality, so expressive—they are really fantastic. To any Italian who reads this, just know that I consider you my friend.

Most of the people in that area were sugarcane growers. One of my church elders was an Italian man of small stature. Everybody was afraid of him because he would start a conversation about religion wherever he went. Whether the subject was the latest news or the weather, he never took long to find a way to bring the Bible into the conversation.

One time he got together with another Italian family of farmers in the same area and really pushed and pressed them about committing their lives to God. Finally, to get him off their backs, they said, "Look, it seems as if you are right, but we need one more thing to resolve this. You're going to bring your pastor; we are going to bring our priest. And they will talk in front of us. You're not going to say a word; just let your pastor talk. We are not going to say anything either. Do you agree?"

They probably thought, *The pastor will surely have fewer ways to defend himself than this fellow,* because he seemed to have all the answers.

And he immediately said, "Yes, of course, I agree."

"You agree to say nothing?"

"I agree to say nothing. My pastor will do all the talking."

So pretty soon he came and said to me, "Pastor, I've gotten you in trouble, but you'll forgive me, won't you?"

I said, "Luis, I have forgiven you so many times already. What difference does one more time make?"

"Good! I was sure you wouldn't mind." And then he explained the situation.

"It's not the first time you've gotten me into something like this," I said. "Of course I'll go."

And it really wasn't the first time, nor was it the last, because this fellow was always talking to people about Jesus.

We arrived about a half hour before the appointed time. I never like to arrive late—or even just on time—for such occasions, because whoever gets there early is owner of the field, whereas the person who comes in late or last has to start by making excuses.

So we sat for a while, talking about this and that. We had to talk about trivial things, of course, because we couldn't talk about what we were going to discuss.

Suddenly the priest's car drove into the farmyard, and everything was astir. The dogs barked, the children shouted, and the people who were working in the house scurried around. Everyone knew the priest had arrived.

The door opened, and he came in. I stood up to greet him, and everyone else stood up as well. As the priest entered, I looked at him closely. He stopped for a few seconds, looking intently right back at me. Then he said, "Is that you, Mario?"

And I said, "You haven't changed at all."

He answered, "You're mistaken. I've changed a lot."

"What do you do here?" I asked him.

"I am the assistant to the parish priest. And you?"

"I am the Adventist pastor in this area."

Then he came over, embraced me, and said, "Brother, I have never forgotten our conversation."

The family was in a total state of shock and suspense; nobody could understand a thing. My little church elder seemed as if he were about to burst.

This man and I then sat down and had a conversation that lasted more or less 15 minutes, about pleasant things and about good relations. Then he stood up. "They told me," he said, addressing the family, "that you wanted a conversation between a priest and an Adventist pastor." Then, looking at me, he said, "I didn't know you were an Adventist pastor." Speaking again to the family, he said, "Anyway, this conversation is not necessary. You are in good hands here. Do whatever this man tells you. As for me, I have nothing more to say, and I'll be on my way."

He shook hands with the people, then came over and gave me another fervent embrace, and said in my ear, "When I get my own parish, I'll invite you." And he left.

There was a moment of total silence. No one said a word. Then my Italian brother couldn't stand it any longer. He turned to the family and said to them, "So . . . what do you say?"

The head of the family, who was Italian, answered, "What more is there to say? Of course we're with you!"

Mario Veloso was a young pastor in Argentina when this experience took place. He later became an administrative secretary at the Adventist world headquarters.

Chapter 3

One in a Million

. . . .

Donald Berry

The author of this story wrote out his experience on a spiral-bound notebook because he has a burden to share with others and encourage someone who might be passing through a similar experience. He wants to assure them that God really cares and can make a difference in their lives.

Drugs are not only an addiction but also a business, and I was deeply involved in both when I had a strange experience. I dreamed that I was sitting in my van on the side of a dark road. My father was sitting with me on my right. I looked, and I saw police cars at either end of the van with all their lights on. They had opened all the doors and were searching for drugs and any other evidence that would make a good case against me. Somehow I realized I was handcuffed with my hands behind my back. With my fingertips I was reaching for my wallet, which had my "business" papers in it. I repeatedly tried to toss it back into the darkness behind me, but I could not get it free from my hands. I then looked at my father and noticed that he was very sad and hurt. He would not look up. He just sat there silently with his head down.

I awoke from my sleep in a cold sweat. It was early morning, and I decided to get up. As I went into my kitchen, I met my friend, whom I'll call Bob. Bob and his girlfriend had been staying at my house while they looked for an apartment. He had come downstairs at the same time I had come into the kitchen. He had a worried look on his face, and I asked him what was wrong.

"I just had a dream that we were cleaning out your house," he said, "and getting rid of all the drugs and paraphernalia. But afterward you got arrested anyway!"

I was shocked. I told him about my own dream. We quickly decided to take action. We cleaned the house of all the drugs we could find and of all related materials. We took everything to a safe place—well, I should say *almost* everything. I still had to have some pot with me, and one small rock of cocaine.

Bob and I talked it over and decided that it was in everyone's best interest for us all to split up. My girlfriend was to go over to my sister's house; Bob and his girlfriend were going skiing for the weekend; and I would simply sit in the house and wait for the police to arrive—if they really were going to arrive.

As I sat in the silence of my home, I thought about everything that had happened to me in the past five years. I wondered where I would have been and what I would have been doing now if it weren't for the drugs. I figured I would more than likely still be in karate, but I would be running my own school by now, doing what I really enjoyed.

Every addict remembers his or her first experience with drugs. Like most others, I said I would just check it out and would never allow myself to get caught in the snare. It's amazing how fast it all happened, and I was sucked into a cesspool of addiction and, before long, dealing.

Someone once said, "It's easy to quit smoking. I've quit a thousand times." I used to give this testimony myself, because it was true for me. How often, in my own strength, had I "quit" smoking, drinking, and snorting cocaine (not to mention all the other things I was doing), only to follow the resolution with an almost immediate return to indulgence! Those of you who have had the experience of trying to quit using something that is mentally or physically addictive certainly know what I am talking about.

When someone tries to quit "cold turkey," he or she will end up with a heavy head, an upset stomach, shakes, and horrible nightmares—if there is any sleep at all. And worst of all, you don't know how long the agony will last.

Often when I tried to quit a particular drug, I found it easy when I replaced it with another. For example, I would replace depressants with antidepressants, marijuana with cocaine. As time went on, in spite of my attempts and even complaints to God, instead of getting free from my problems, I would sink deeper.

My girlfriend felt the same way. One time I found her in bed curled up like a ball. Her whole body was shaking, and with great sobs she said, "It's just that I hate it so much, but I love it too!"

The drug business works on the basis of friendships. You know someone, and that person introduces you to someone else, and these connections are how things move. A friend I will call Phil connected me with two other guys who opened the way for me to have much more "success." One day they called and told me they wanted to buy five pounds of cocaine! Five pounds! That amount represented about $100,000 to $115,000 at that time. I would make a profit of between $30,000 to $50,000 on that deal alone.

The very night after making this deal I had the dream I described at the beginning. I was sitting there in my house thinking about all of this, when the phone rang. I answered and heard the voice of John, one of the two friends who wanted to buy the five pounds of cocaine. He asked me if I had the cocaine ready for delivery.

"No," I said. "But wait. Someone's at the door."

"You don't have any for me?" he shouted.

"No, John, I don't. I'm trying to quit the business and the drugs because it's just getting too nerve-racking for me. But wait just a second. Someone's at my door."

As I laid down the phone to answer the door, my heart was beating faster and harder than it ever had before. As I approached the door, I suddenly noticed that it wasn't just a loud knock. Someone was trying to kick the door down!

"Hold on! I'll open it!" I yelled.

The pounding stopped for a second, but when I unlatched the deadbolt, the door was kicked again, and it flew open, hitting me in the face and knocking me to the floor. Before I could get up, a police officer was crouching over me shoving a 12-gauge shotgun into my mouth.

"So much as breathe wrong, and your brains will be all over the floor," he shouted. I didn't move, but all I could think of was *Do I really want to live anyway?*

Almost instantly the house was filled with police officers, detectives, and photographers. While I lay on the floor, John, one of my "friends," came in. To my surprise, it turned out that John was a very good undercover narcotics task force agent. I say "very good" because he looked like a hippie and had me fooled all the way. He did his job the way it should be done, although I sure didn't thank him for it at the time.

After ransacking my house and finding my little stash of pot but no cocaine, they realized I had expected them.

"Who tipped you off?" they asked.

"God," I said. "He warned me in a dream."

I got nothing but snide remarks from the police when I told them that. When we got to jail, they told me that my friend, who was next up the dealer's ladder from me, was in the same boat. *Oh no!* I thought to myself. Until now I had had hopes he would bail me out.

I was arrested at 8:00 on a Friday night. It was a bad winter, and I was very cold in the jail. I didn't see a blanket until morning. Since Monday was a holiday, I had to wait until Tuesday to be arraigned.

My cell was about five feet by eight feet. The bed was a quarter inch of steel—and I'm not talking about springs, but a solid sheet of steel. The bed had no mattress, only one blanket, and no pillow. The toilet in the rear of the cell was in full view of the cameras that watched everything I did. In jail no privacy exists, other than what's in your mind. My cell was against the wall of the police garage, and I could hear patrol cars coming in and out all night long. I don't think the garage door was shut very often, if at all. I asked one of the officers if I could get another blanket, because I could see my breath all too easily, and the steel bed was very cold.

I didn't see another blanket until morning, but I realize now that they were only trying to break down my sense of being somebody; now I was just another number to them and a criminal to society.

At the court on Tuesday it was no better. I was informed of the charges against me. Each count in the act of selling cocaine carried a maximum of 15 years, and the sale of marijuana had a maximum of seven years. In total I was looking at a maximum of 82 years. With that possibility in front of me, suicide was a constant thought of escape. I pleaded not guilty, and the judge set my bail at $100,000.

My lawyer asked if it could be lowered, but the judge was adamant. "No way!" he said. "I know these cocaine dealers. If I lower the bail, he will be out of the country by next week."

Nevertheless, with some extra pleading on the part of my lawyer, the judge lowered it to $75,000. I needed 10 percent of that to post bail. Because of my addiction, I was broke. I knew my parents would be willing to help me, but they didn't have that kind of money and neither did my sister. It seemed there was no hope of getting out now. The next stop would be an extremely dangerous prison.

In spite of all I had done, the Lord was there working on my behalf, which is something I still can't understand. It just so "happened" that one of my uncles was in the courtroom talking with his friend, who was a bondsperson. When my uncle saw me, he asked his friend if he could help and convinced the man that it would be a safe investment; I would certainly come back to court for sentencing. So the bondsperson lowered the price for bail from 10 percent to 4.5 percent. That brought it down from $7,500 to $3,375. My sister had come to the arraignment, and she now hurried to the bank to take out a loan. When she arrived, it was already closed, but in her desperation she knocked anyway. To her surprise, a friend of hers answered the door and let her in!

"What are you doing here?" my sister asked.

"I'm a loan officer at this bank. How can I help you?"

Can you imagine? My sister not only got the loan that night, but got it in cash as well!

Before long the guards came and called me. What a surprise it was when, instead of assigning me to a cell, they took me to a meeting room, and there were my siser and my parents, who had come back from another state to be there for me!

The ride home was very quiet but not without love and prayers. It had been so very long since we had all been together and I hadn't been in a hurry to leave their company so I could go get high. But this time was different.

When we got to my sister's home, my girlfriend greeted me with many tears and open arms, which, to me, meant more than just a welcome. After being away from her for the past five days, I knew I didn't want to live without her, and soon after that I asked her if she would be my wife.

But settling in at my sister's house was not easy. I had many severe periods of paranoia that made it impossible to relax even a little. Some of my worries may have been mere hallucinations, while others came from a more tangible threat to my safety. In my mind I was guilty of many a crime, but did the police know any more than they let on? Were they still searching for more evidence to convict me on other sales? Every night I had the most hellish nightmares.

Once morning came and everyone gathered for breakfast, I would join in, but I was still very moody from all that had been going on in my mind. I found I was extremely on edge, snapping at everyone and getting very angry over the littlest things. The paranoia I experienced at that time was overwhelming. I figured there were plenty of good reasons to worry about nearly everything. Little did I know that these were some of the symptoms of withdrawal from the many types of drugs that were still in my system. It takes days for many of them to leave your system.

At times I would pick up the phone and yell into it violently, thinking that the police were probably listening to every word. I also figured that the house was bugged, so I often walked through the house yelling into the TV or radio or any other electronic device that could transmit or be a power source.

Of course, my family was alarmed at the way I was acting. My sister had started going to Bible studies and attending an Adventist church, and she decided to ask if two young men from her church would stop by. The two men, whom I will refer to as Dave and Ray, agreed to stop by and talk with me in hopes of being helpful. I can't remember how she asked me, and I don't remember my immediate response, but I agreed to give them one hour. If I didn't like what they had to say, I thought to myself, it would be a short hour.

Now, as the enemy of my soul would have it, a close friend named Bryant stopped by and asked me if I wanted to go on a short ride in the country "just to relax."

"Man, you seem real nervous!" he said as soon as we were alone. "Here, I brought something that will calm you down so much that you'll forget what your trouble was."

"Like what?" I asked.

As I looked, he pulled out a joint. "Panama Red," he exclaimed. He was smiling from ear to ear, thinking he was doing me a big favor.

Like the fool I was I quickly said, "All right. Light it up."

I did, in fact, smoke that weed and began to feel relaxed and peaceful in a way I hadn't felt in a long time.

I returned home, thanked Bryant for the "nice ride," and away he went. Now the reality of the moment hit me like a ton of bricks. I was relaxed, smelled like smoke, and was high as a kite, and—on top of it all—Ray and Dave were coming in about one hour. Needless to say, I didn't want them to know I was high. So, trying to act as normal as possible, I went in and washed up. Then to help my breath, I ate something and sat down.

My parents knew that I was on something, but they didn't mention it then for many reasons—one reason being that if they got me upset, I would probably not listen to what Dave and Ray had to say. It was the first time in days I'd been so relaxed, and they knew a simple ride in the country couldn't have done that, nor would a simple ride make my nose run or my eyes so red and glassy.

All was quiet in my sister's home until we heard Dave and Ray drive up to the house.

"Oh, boy, I hope these guys aren't going to give me the holier-than-thou routine," I exclaimed.

I must admit that at the time I was not the nicest person, and it was mainly because of my appearance. I was dressed nearly always in old blue jeans. I don't think I had more than three haircuts in the course of year. My beard matched the rest of my head—long and shaggy—and if I didn't like somebody, I wouldn't hesitate to let them know.

After introductions we all sat down and broke the ice with small talk. It was then that I looked them over. They seemed to be well-mannered and neatly dressed. In fact, to my surprise, they didn't seem to act as if they were superior to me or have a holier-than-thou attitude. I must also add that when they finished speaking with my parents and sister and turned to me, their facial expressions remained the same: happy, peaceful, and, if I'm not mistaken, loving. This was a look I had experienced only with my family and my girlfriend. But now here were two guys I'd never seen before, and they seemed to care about me and the situation I had gotten myself into. They offered me hope where there was none and courage when it could not be found. Everything they said was filled with sincerity and truth. And all of it came from the Word of God.

Not only did I listen to what Dave and Ray said, but I soaked it up with gladness. And when the hour was up, I asked them if they would stay longer! After they left, my family and I all talked for hours and went to bed feeling strengthened and filled with hope. I felt remorse for having been so high when they came, but I knew I couldn't go back and change my actions.

That night it seemed as though I was asleep before my head hit the pillow, but it also seemed that no more than 15 minutes went by before I awoke from another nightmare. This time I dreamed I was being arrested because of that stinking half ounce I had tucked away. So out it came. I added a few pennies to the baggie for weight and flushed it down the toilet. I felt a sense of relief, and I went back to bed and had a great night's sleep.

A couple of weeks passed. I was living back at my parents' house, and they were still supportive of me. But I was having trouble giving up smoking. Oh, how I wish now that I had thrown everything away, but in my desire to cling to my cherished sin of smoking, at times I made it difficult—if not impossible—for the Lord to bless me or to draw as close as He desired. It could have been over so quickly, but I dragged it out for so long that it seemed almost impossible to quit.

Anyway, I continued to see Dave and Ray on a weekly basis. I also asked for more frequent study from the pastor of their church. He was a nice man, recently a widower, who was now even more excited about the Lord's return because of the promise of seeing his wife again. We were enjoying our studies on the books of Daniel and Revelation so much that my parents asked to join in.

My strength was increasing every day, and I tried to encourage my friends to quit dealing drugs and join me in the studies. Some quit for a little while, but they didn't want "that religious stuff." I plainly remember Bryant saying to me, "There are two things I never talk about with anyone: politics and religion." How sad it is that many people have this attitude, for with it they shut out the possibility of hearing the truth, maybe even for the last time.

It was just shy of one month after my arrest that I received news of Bryant's death. My cousin got news at the police department where she worked. She came over early in the morning and made the announcement in the presence of my whole family.

Looking straight at me, she said, "Bryant is dead."

At that, I turned and walked away, not saying a word. After reaching my bedroom, I fell to my knees and cried bitterly. He had been shot in the chest with a small-caliber rifle—clean through the heart. Whether it was murder, accident, or suicide, to this day no one really knows. This is the drug world, my friends, the real drug world. Not some fantasyland where nothing ever goes wrong, but a world in which lives are ruined if not totally destroyed.

There had been another incident when I had stopped in to see Kenny, the guy who was up from me on the dealers' ladder, and found him leaving with another guy I'll call Angelo. Both were very mad and in a rush. When I asked what was wrong, Kenny said tersely, "Somebody thinks he's going to get away with something—but he's not! We've got a bill to collect!"

With guns in hand and in their shoulder holsters, off they went. A couple days later I picked up the paper and found out that Angelo had been shot to death. Both he and his car had been riddled with hundreds of bullets. It was considered a gangland killing, and the case was closed. Of course I don't know how much Kenny may have been involved, but I think you can see my point.

I tried to prepare myself for what was ahead, but it was very hard. Every so often my father reminded me that during the war it was a common thing to be away from family for five or six years. So I tried to consider my impending jailtime like going away to war or something.

Meanwhile, an opportunity came up for me to go to school and to also get paid minimum wage for it, so I took it. It sounded rather dumb at first. I was now beginning a career on the bottom level of the food service industry as a cook. But for some reason I loved it. Everything started to turn around.

Only five months after my arrest, I married Cyndy. Ray and Dave's pastor performed the ceremony. By that time Cyndy and I were going to Ray and Dave's church on a weekly basis, and our Bible studies were still going strong. They were getting so interesting that we felt we just couldn't get enough.

Neither Cyndy nor I had graduated from high school, so we studied and took our GEDs. We both passed and received our equivalency diplomas. Soon we both decided we wanted to be baptized into the church we had grown to love so very much, and we reached that goal only eight months after my arrest.

At the beginning of my court case, I pleaded innocent on the grounds of addiction. But now I decided to change my plea to guilty and to throw myself on the mercy of court. I informed my lawyer of my decision to plead guilty, and the court date was set. I will be the first to admit that although I changed my plea because I felt the conviction of the Holy Spirit, I was still afraid of what was going to happen inside the courtroom. As I said before, I had a very good lawyer. He said he was positive I was going to serve a minimum of five years, although he was hoping for less.

"I'm very glad to see you change your plea," he said. "You didn't really have any chance fighting it, and they could have given you a stiffer sentence had you chosen to fight. I've noticed that you and your family have become quite religiously minded over all this, so now my advice to you is to pray to your Friend upstairs. After all, you never can tell. Maybe He can help a little." Well, my lawyer didn't have to tell me that. I knew that God was my "refuge and strength, a very present help in trouble" (Ps. 46:1).

The court proceeding turned out to be long and aggravating, but God was in complete control. I attended not only my first court appointment but also my second, third, fourth, and fifth, and so on. My sentencing was canceled and postponed so many times that I lost count, but the Lord was not sleeping. He was working on my behalf in all of this. At least a couple of times my lawyer said, "I don't know what you've been praying for exactly, but keep it up, because something's happening."

Something *was* happening. The Lord was working in our lives. Before I was arrested, my long hair matched my beard very well. My language was as dirty as my clothing. As I went from one court case to another and the months slipped by, the Lord continued to clean up my life. I know that for the sake of His name and His glory He opened the eyes of both the judge and prosecutor to notice the month-by-month changes in my appearance—physically, mentally, and spiritually. My lawyer said I had to be pointed out to the judge because he couldn't recognize me from the way I had first appeared. And now he wanted dated information on my case for his review. My lawyer mentioned that the judge could hardly believe I had sold cocaine at one time.

My first paid vacation finally arrived, and it happened to fall on the week of camp meeting, so we decided to attend. "Camp meeting" is a time all who wish to can come to a special campground for about 10 days and stay in tents or their vans or campers for the purpose of attending the meetings. A sanctuary or large auditorium is in the midst of all the tents. I was looking forward to my first camp meeting and to fellowshipping with my friends and family in Christ.

It was the day before we were to leave for camp meeting, and I was checking the oil on my van in preparation for the trip when I heard the phone ringing. I raced inside to answer it, but on the other end was the last person I wanted to talk to at the time—my lawyer.

"Well, this is it," he said. "You're going to be sentenced tomorrow."

My heart fell about as low as my stomach. "Is there any possibility that it might be postponed?" I asked.

"No. I doubt it. Why?" he said.

"Well, my wife and I just started our first paid vacation, and we were going to go to our annual church camp meeting for a week," I explained. There was silence for a moment.

"Well, you plan on being there anyway," he said. "If there are any changes on my end, I'll call you. If I don't talk to you, I'll see you in my office at 8:00 a.m. tomorrow."

As soon as we hung up, I knelt down and prayed. I pleaded with the Lord to allow me to go to camp meeting to receive the strength I needed to accept the long prison term I was facing. I also asked the Lord to soften the hearts of those who were in power over me, and if it was in His will, to even show mercy. I then called a small number of church members to whom I was especially close and asked them to pray for me also.

Within a couple of hours my lawyer called and told me the sentencing had been postponed for one more week! "But one week only," he said. "It will definitely be on Friday. So have a good time and keep on praying. I'll see you then."

"Praise God!" I exclaimed. So I finished packing, and off we went.

The whole week was filled with precious moments of joy and reminiscing. I treasured my last moments of freedom. In the past I had taken it for granted, but it was now more valued than gold. Each time I hugged or kissed my wife, each time I shook a friend's hand, I wondered how many more times I would have that pleasure. It felt as if life itself was slipping away from me. At times I became very depressed, but not for long, for the Lord was my constant strength. It often felt as if He picked me up and carried me.

Toward the middle of the week a dear soul who knew the trouble I was in made an announcement to the crowd of about 3,000 Christian believers present at the meeting that I needed prayer. He mentioned that prayers would be needed especially on Friday. Throughout the remaining time people I didn't know would stop me just to say, "I don't know you, brother, or what your troubles may be, but I'll be praying for you."

I ask you: is this true brotherly love? I believe it is. Caring for souls around you: isn't this what the Lord taught? "Pray one for another."

On Friday at 8:00 a.m. I was ready to go to court with my wife and parents to receive the sentence. The lawyer told us he was certain the sentence would be only 20 years. Furthermore, if we could come up with another $5,000, we could appeal it.

"No," I said. "Not only can I not afford it, but I also trust the Lord will have it His way no matter what." We all went to the courthouse, and my lawyer told us to take a seat. He then said he would be back in time for my sentencing.

In a very short time the courtroom began to fill up. There were many others being seated who were also waiting for their cases to come up. Every time the doors opened I hoped to see a familiar face, and soon I spotted Ray coming through the doors.

This was a great relief to me, for he was a great support for my spiritual well-being. We had prayer and read many scriptures that gave me hope, trust, and strength in the Lord. Though I was expecting my lawyer, I was hoping to see another friend. *But why keep looking?* I thought. *No one else is coming.* So I put the thought out of my mind and kept on studying and praying and telling my wife how much I loved her.

Suddenly I felt a hand on my shoulder. I assumed it belonged to my lawyer, but when I turned, to my happy surprise it was my pastor.

"Good morning," he said with a cheerful voice. "How's your courage?"

With tears of great joy and nearly ready to burst at the surprise, I exclaimed, "Right now, much better! But I'm still a bit nervous."

"That's expected," he answered with a calm, trusting voice.

"But you are so busy at the camp meeting! How did you manage to get away?" I asked.

And again with a calmness that comes from being well acquainted with the peace and the love of God, my pastor answered, "Well, just after I talked to you this morning, I called your lawyer and asked him if he thought it would be helpful if I were present for your sentencing. He replied with a definite yes. So I reasoned that if I was to be here in time, I had no time to waste. I made some quick arrangements to have my positions covered at camp meeting, and I was on my way. I must add that the Lord is good, for He opened the way, and there was little traffic the whole way here." Needless to say, my family and I could hardly express our relief and happiness to see him there.

Several more cases came up then, and it seemed as though Satan was there also to cast doubt before me that even Jesus Himself would not be able to help me. I witnessed a young man barely out of his teens who was convicted of selling $20 worth of cocaine to an undercover agent receive five to 15 years at a state prison. Whether or not he had had a previous record I didn't know, but for a 19-year-old kid, that seemed pretty stiff to me.

Then I saw three young men. One had been proved to be mentally retarded, another was the driver, and the third had killed a man with a wine bottle and a rock during a robbery for $20 or $30. The first young man received 15 years, the second 25 years, and the third 38 years, and none of them were out of their teens!

Then I watched another 19-year-old get one year for breaking probation, and the judge said he was going to be nice to him. I thought to myself, *If he is nice to me, I'll get 35 years, and if he isn't, I'll get 65 or maybe even more.*

At last my lawyer arrived, and my name was soon called. Physically, I stood before the judge, but spiritually I was kneeling before Him who judges the world.

In the past few cases I had witnessed, I noticed that after the case was presented by both sides, the judge always asked the prosecuting attorney what the state had recommended for punishment. If the prosecutor recommended 15 years, the judge would give 15 years. If the prosecutor recommended 38 years, the judge would give 38, and so on.

Now, the prosecutor stated the extent of the crimes I had committed. But on request of recommended punishment, he quickly looked over his papers and then made his statement: "Your Honor, although this man has committed the previous crimes, he has kept out of trouble ever since, and at this time the state has no recommendation." That was all.

Next, my lawyer asked if the judge wouldn't mind a testimony from my pastor.

"If you think it will help the court in a proper decision," the judge replied, "then please proceed."

"Yes, sir, Your Honor, I do," my lawyer answered.

Then my pastor gave a wonderful testimony on my behalf. At its close he added, "Your Honor, if it were possible, I would gladly take any responsibility needed to ensure his release. I believe that although he may have been a criminal at one time, he is now a changed person and, therefore, no longer a threat to society."

As the pastor finished, my lawyer whispered in my ear and said, "The judge will ask you if you want to say anything on your own behalf. When you speak, start and stop everything you say with 'sir.'"

"OK," I replied, but the nervousness of the past two years of waiting came upon on me all at once.

"Son," the judge asked me, "do you have anything to say before I pronounce your sentence?"

"Uh . . . yes, uh . . . ," I replied with trembling voice before proceeding. "You see, I realize now that what I did was wrong, although I didn't realize it at first. I also know that I deserve worse than what you'll give me, for I know I deserve nothing less than death. But now I've discovered what life is really all about. Every morning I feel as if God has blessed me with another chance. I've gone to school and learned to cook, and I actually love my job. I've gotten married and have a wonderful wife who loves me. Before, my family and I had drifted apart, but now we're closer than ever. I found a church that I love and people there I can love and trust like my own family. In fact, my whole family is now closer to God than ever, and I guess for that alone it was all worth it. And, well, I guess that's it."

In my state of shock I had forgotten all about starting and finishing with "sir." On occasion I noticed the judge looking past me in the direction of my family. Later I found out that they were either in tears or praying or both. With all these elements combined, he made his decision. He looked at me with a very sober look on his face and said, "I see no way other than incarceration for this type of crime." Then, looking at me and the others in the courtroom, he said, "Did you know that everyone who walks through those doors into this courtroom claims that they have 'changed' and that none of them will ever do anything bad again? But," he continued, "as I have heard this one case and seen it progress, I am convinced it is genuine. It is one in a million." And now he looked at the rest of those in the courtroom and said, "Now, don't any of you think this will happen again. As I said, this is one in a million."

Then his attention came back to me, and he continued, while shaking his head as if what he was about to say was not what he was wanting to say: "As I said before, I'll say again. I see no way other than incarceration for this type of crime . . . but I'm not going to incarcerate you."

My heart nearly jumped out of my chest for joy and relief, realizing how my wife, family, and dearest friends had stood behind me. Later I found out from my family (for my eyes and attention had been fixed on the judge) that all the court-appointed help looked at one another in utter amazement at the judge's words.

"However," the judge continued, "you will be required, at the end of or during this workweek, to pay a fine of $1,500 to this court and an additional $1,500 to a drug rehabilitation center. The payments must be proven by means of a receipt. In addition to this, you will serve 500 hours free community service. It is my judgment that you will be given a five-year suspended sentence, and you will also serve a three-year probation, during which time, if you are convicted of any crime other than traffic violations, you will serve the full term set by this court.

"And now I would like to add: Son, you have some very special friends and a nice family. *Don't disappoint them.*"

That evening I had the immense joy of returning to camp meeting to share with everyone present the incredible way the Lord had intervened in my life. I reassured them that Jesus Christ wants to give freedom, peace, and permanent joy not only to me but to everyone.

Friend, before I finish this story I want to ask you a question, and I hope you won't misunderstand. Is there any area of your life you would like to change? If you feel the need to change or know someone who needs it, will you simply read this story and put it aside and go on with your life as usual? With all my heart, I hope not.

First of all, you need to *ask.* Seek God for help, and I don't mean just saying the words but asking with all your heart. The Bible talks about "fervent prayer" (Acts 12:5; James 5:16). It says that "during the days of Jesus' life on earth, he offered up prayers and petitions with fervent cries and tears" (Heb. 5:7, NIV). So how can anyone believe that we, who are great sinners, need only to repeat a routine prayer once in a while without feeling any special need or sense of urgency?

If we cry out to God with all our hearts and ask Him for renewal, His promise is sure: "Ask and it will be given to you; seek and you will find; knock and the door will be opened to you. For everyone who asks receives; the one who seeks finds; and to the one who knocks, the door will be opened" (Luke 11:9, 10, NIV). And it says, "Whoever comes to me I will never drive away" (John 6:37, NIV). Never doubt that He will accept you; He longs to receive you as His son or daughter.

Allow me also to recommend that if you do not have a church connection, try to find one as soon as possible. Don't think the people you will find in church are a bunch of super saints. They are normal people made of flesh and blood just like you and me. They know what it is to struggle against sin and temptation. But if you give them a chance, they will gladly offer you their friendship, their prayers, and their counsel. Please, for your own sake, for the eternal good of your soul, connect yourself with a strong church body without delay.

In addition to churches, there are many social agencies that specialize in offering help to those who want to overcome addictions. You can find many sites on the Internet that offer help.

And now I leave you with this one last word: Never doubt that God loves you. No matter how far you have gone, if you really want to change, He will be there for you, and He will never, ever leave you.

Chapter 4

A Lost Cause

Pat Grant

The circulation of blood in my brother's brain had obviously stopped. He had lost all comprehension of the word "no."

AJ had been persistent in inviting me, as had my father, but the idea of church and a belief in God wasn't for me. I had been to church as a kid, at least whenever my mother could find the strength to take us after working night shift as a nurse; now I was on my own. I made my own decisions, and I had decided that God was obsolete.

"Why not?" he asked as we sat in our shared living space.

"All right, O stubborn one, let me explain." I pointed at him. "We come from a divorced home. There was a lot of pain during those times. God was never there. I don't remember Him ever being there. If you want to believe in God, hey, that's wonderful. If you want to look to the sky, hold your hands high, and sing 'In the sweet by and by,' great! I'll stay a little more grounded, you ninny." (I can't tell you what I really called him.)

"Come with me to church once, and I'll never bother you again about God, salvation, or religion," he said.

My kid brother's words hinted of sweet release. "Let's make sure I understand you. I go to church with you on *uno*—three minus two equals one—occasion, and in return I never hear you ask, beg, request, invite, or so much as look at me holy again. Right?"

"Right."

"You got a deal," I chortled with my arms in the air in mock praise. "But there's one condition: If I'm going to church with you, I'm going exactly the way I am."

"Deal," he replied.

"Amen, brother; looks like we're going to church."

Sabbath morning came. My brother was garbed in his pressed slacks, shoes that glinted of preciseness, and a tie of impeccable fashion. He wafted a whisper of cologne that riveted my olfactory senses.

I also was properly dressed—according to my attitude. I had put in my best gold earrings, two in one ear, one in the other. I wore my favorite frayed jeans, black boots, and a black leather biking jacket. I, too, had a whisper of something on, but it smelled more like bad breath. I crafted my hair into a dome that resembled a mushroom cloud after Chernobyl. I was ready for this day—very ready. If I knew anything about church people, I thought that if I didn't look like them or smell like them, they would leave me alone!

We got into the car and drove to my brother's church. I was defensive, circumspect, and eager to fulfill my part of the agreement. We walked into the building, and immediately people came up to me and shook my hand. *Yeah,* I thought, *I'm not stupid. My brother prepped you for my arrival.* I shook hands, stared icily, and projected nonverbal signals that I wasn't interested. There would be no conversion here.

The service was vibrant, the songs gripping, and the atmosphere a euphony of praise and worship. But I felt stifled. *There's nothing in the world worth being this happy about,* I thought. *I'm in a room full of maniacs.*

The preacher, Roscoe Howard, animated in his style and passionate in his delivery, thundered, "Please turn to this verse in your Bibles," he thundered. The crinkle of pages suffused the room. I sat quietly and glanced at my watch. Fifteen more minutes and this would be over.

"Hey, mister," someone whispered.

At first I didn't look. I thought he was talking to someone else.

"Mister; you don't have a Bible."

He couldn't have been more than 10. I later learned that his name was Ceddaric Collins.

"No, kid; I don't have a Bible," I replied.

"Hey, mister, what's your name?"

"If I tell you my name, will you leave me alone?"

"Maybe."

"My name is Pat, Pat Grant. Now listen to the preacher; you might learn something."

Ceddaric then took out a blue Bic pen with a clear plastic barrel, opened the cover of his white-bound King James Version Bible, and wrote my name in it. "Here," he said as he handed it to me.

I looked over to see him holding out his Bible. "Here, this is for you. You look like you need a Bible."

"I don't want this, kid. You keep it."

"Naw, I want you to have it; so take it." He thrust it into my hand.

I remained quiet and listened to the rest of the sermon.

After the service was over, I blazed a path to the car, got in, and waited for my brother.

"So whaddya think?" he asked me when he finally arrived.

"I hated it," I replied. "Look, if you want this God thing, fine. It's not for me. A deal's a deal. I kept my end; now get off my back."

We sat in silence for the remainder of the ride home.

As soon as we got home I began preparing to go to the library. I had to finish an assignment that was due Monday morning. There was one problem: I didn't know what to do with the Bible the kid had given me. My name was written in it with 10-year-old chicken scratch, and I couldn't bring myself to throw it away. I placed it on the refrigerator and left the house.

Later that evening, after I arrived home, I went to get something to eat. The Bible was sitting there, right where I had left it. It bothered me seeing it there, so I moved it to the living room. The next day I went to watch TV, and there it was, so I moved it back to the kitchen. Each day I moved the Bible from one room to another room to another. I just wanted it anywhere I wasn't.

Late Thursday evening I spread out my textbooks in my bedroom to study, when I saw the Bible sitting on my dresser. Rain had formed droplets on my window, and light from the streetlights filtered through. The refracted rays on that Bible sprayed a shadow of light and darkness that seemed to vie for my attention.

I focused on that white King James Bible and remembered the little hands that had given it to me. A thick slab of silence hung in my room. A din of discomfort screamed in my soul, asking questions I couldn't answer. *What possessed that kid to give me his Bible?*

Then more questions flooded my mind. *Pat, what is the meaning of life? Is this all there is? Is this all you have to look forward to, only more of the same degradation you've already been through? If Jesus Christ doesn't exist, if He is an ethereal myth, why do you hate Him?*

The questions persisted, and I had no answers. I was running from something I didn't know anything about. I walked over to my brother's bedroom.

"Yeah?" he said, when he saw me standing at the door.

"I, uh . . . listen, don't flip out on me. Don't preach—or even smile."

"What?"

"I've got a few questions. I'm not interested in being religious or anything, but I do have a few things I need explained. If you can find me someone to talk to, I'd like to know more about God."

My brother smiled.

A year and a half later I was baptized. Since then a lot has happened in my life. I'm a pastor. What was once hate is now love. What was once disbelief is now faith. That is the power of God.

I stand in awe, unable to speak
    that a Man who has power would be gentle and meek
    and condescend to me
    so that I might see
    that the life I was living
    was never meant to be.
For the rest of my days I will take up His cause,
    and even now I must stop daily
    just to pause,
    for eternity I will offer applause
    to a God who forgot
    that I was a lost cause.

Chapter 5

Unlikely Lamb

Marco Antonio Huaco

In 1990 I was enrolled at San Marcos University in Lima, Peru. It was an exciting and sometimes dangerous place to be.

San Marcos had long been the throbbing intellectual heart of the country, but at that time the country and its universities were convulsed by violence and political unrest as left-wing student organizations fought among themselves and against the government.

I chose to study law, hoping also to gain an understanding of history, politics, and philosophy. It had always seemed to me that the search for truth was not a mere scientific or intellectual exercise. To search for it, to persevere until you stood face to face with the truth that underlies existence itself, based on reason and sense, is a fundamental purpose in life. And in that I was not disappointed. My first years at the university were an exciting time of intellectual discovery.

But my explorations into philosophy and science soon created a conflict between my deeply rooted Catholic faith and my rational inquiry into life and its meaning. I wondered, *Can faith and reason coexist? Can faith be reconciled with science?*

Before long I abandoned all belief in God. The vacuum was filled by an increasing enchantment with the materialistic philosophy of Marxism. In my new way of thinking, the eternal was represented by the continuous evolution of organic matter. The world was the product of a big bang, followed by innumerable evolutionary leaps, which produced all life and consciousness. It was not God who created humans, but vice versa. Christianity was simply one mystic sect among others that happened to become popular through an accident of history.

Unfortunately, I did not meet any Christians during that time who were prepared to refute my arguments. They all attempted to defend God with a priori doctrinal statements that seemed dogmatic and emotional to me.

Around 1991 I wrote: "In a society that is in its death throes, as ours is, in which social struggle is every day more and more dramatic, the masses must give up religious myths and metaphysics and embrace a new faith, a new religion of revolutionary politics."

I soon decided to move from words to action by joining a socialist student organization. As young left-wing activists, we often found ourselves caught in the crossfire between the repressive state and Maoist terrorism.

Christian students were not exempt from the conflict. Because religion was "the opium of the people," they were automatically deemed enemies of the revolution, especially Seventh-day Adventists, who were considered "the face of Yankee imperialism." On one occasion the Adventist students worked very hard to paint a mural of an open Bible on our campus. Two days later they found their handiwork covered with black paint and a red hammer and sickle in the center with the words "Out of San Marcos, swine!"

In 1995, as a sworn Marxist-Leninist with a record of political activism and ideological fever, I was elected secretary general of the student federation for the law school and president of the university's coordinating committee of student organizations.

At this climactic point of political activism I became acquainted with a young woman who was a classmate and an Adventist believer. Burdened as I was with overwhelming responsibilities as a student leader, I often relied on her to take notes and collect syllabi for the classes I was forced to miss. Her unprejudiced and helpful attitude toward one who relentlessly criticized religion and all believers led me to be curious about her "peculiar" beliefs. I could tolerate many of the things she told me, but I nearly laughed in her face when she said that Adventists believe that the devil is a personal being. I also considered it unacceptable that Adventists didn't drink, dance, or smoke. Nor could I accept their fanatical observance of the Jewish Sabbath. But I liked her as a person, so I shrugged it off. *That's just the way things are with the sects,* I told myself.

About that time, the Adventist Student Center sponsored a lecture on biblical archaeology by Adventist scholar Merling Alomía, and my friend timidly asked if I would like to attend. Because of my respect for her and curiosity about differing ideologies, I accepted. I had a pretty good idea he would talk about Jesus and say we need to give Him our hearts or something like that. I was shocked and totally unprepared for what I heard that night.

Alomía offered a carefully reasoned position showing the relationship between faith and science, between the Bible and scientific research. He told us about some ancient scrolls discovered in 1947 near the Dead Sea that contain most of the book of Isaiah and prove with absolute certainty that this prophetic book existed in its present form long before the birth of Jesus.

Sometime before that I had read a book called *Hipótesis sobre Jesús* by Vittorio Messori,* which described an amazing prophecy about the ministry and death of Jesus that is found the book of Isaiah. Now I asked myself, *Were these real predictions that were actually fulfilled?*

That night I did something I would never have done otherwise; I reached to a corner shelf of my personal library and took out a forgotten book—the Bible. With the help of the index, I found the book of Isaiah and turned to chapter 53. I read it again and again, amazed at the harmony between the details described in that prophecy and facts about Jesus' life.

As I sat there meditating, it seemed as if an earthquake was shaking the foundations of my philosophy of history. If something called "prophecy" really existed, it meant that my materialistic house of cards had to come tumbling down. *What sort of "intellect" could foresee the future? Is being (a visible reality) determined by consciousness (God), and not consciousness by being as postulated by Marx and other materialists? What if there really is such a thing?*

My thoughts whirled about in wild confusion. Wasn't I the very public leader of the university's most vocal socialist organization, a proponent of the wave of the future in the student movement? What would my friends think if the militant atheist were to suddenly turn into a meek little lamb and follower of a religious sect? The struggle went on for hours.

What was clear to me was that truth would still be truth regardless of my personal preference and situation. The truth of something does not depend on the number of people who recognize it as such. Also, I would be the one injured if I were to live a life based on self-deception.

Finally I decided to put some of my thoughts on paper. Here is what I wrote that night: "I recall the face of Christ as I have seen it in a picture, and its reality moves my heart to such fear and uncertainty; it brings me face to face with so many questions that I prefer to stop thinking about it. I don't want to blaspheme; I don't want my rationalism to again cloud His pure love for me. I consider it an act of ingratitude to reflect on whether He loves me or doesn't love me, whether I am important to Him or not . . . because He has, in fact, loved me all my life. When I ran away from Him, He drew me back. I prefer to leave it at that. I don't want to wound Him. But I STILL DO NOT BELIEVE IN HIM. I feel as if I am sinking into an absurdity. I am not the same as before. I have completely lost my way. Nothing satisfies me; I don't know where I am headed. Who am I? What should I do to live? At times humanity fills me with such contempt that I am afraid of becoming arrogant. And divinity is so distant that it is hard for me to even imagine becoming a true Christian. Turn the other cheek? Love my enemies? O God, why do You ask me for something that is so impossible?"

I concluded it would be best for me to remain calm and reach a good decision. I told myself, "You've got to reopen this idea of the existence of God. Research it. Go back to square one." No end of questions churned in my mind. If God exists, how can we account for so much injustice and exploitation? How can we talk about a merciful God if He is indifferent to pain? Why was the Inquisition victorious for centuries, when many of the martyrs were on God's side? I couldn't understand. I only knew that Isaiah 53 and Psalm 22 existed centuries before they were perfectly fulfilled by the facts. In the biblical account even the Pharisees never questioned the reality of Jesus' miracles, only His authority to perform them. I could see, as in a dream, a serene and smiling face, somewhat youthful but mature. That was a momentous night! The Saul within me fell to the earth and his wisdom rolled in the dust.

I kept to myself the grave doubts I still had about the Christian faith. I asked questions; I debated with my comrades; I read constantly; I opened the Bible, searching. I was astounded that most of the so-called freethinkers around me wanted to skip over some fundamental facts out of fear of the truth or out of simple prejudice.

It was at this point that I was invited to join a small group that was studying the topic of justification by faith in the Bible. I discovered that a Christian is not someone who has achieved a certain grade of moral perfection; the Christian life is a friendship with Jesus. And through this friendship we grow to be more like Him. I realized then that the "opium" Marx talked about cannot be identified with the true religion of the Bible.

About that time there was a week of preaching by Pastor Alejandro Bullón. This coincided with a very important crisis and political struggle, and it seemed nearly impossible to attend, but I persevered and was able to attend one meeting. The topic that night was the conversion of Saul. It was overwhelming! Had the Holy Spirit led me there just to speak to me? In a daze, I left the auditorium and hailed a taxi to go home. To my surprise, as we rolled along through the darkened streets, the driver turned to me and asked, "Do you know the Lord Jesus?"

Trembling, I said, "Yes, I think I do, now."

The following year, 1996, was difficult for me. Because of my political activism, the authorities expelled me from the university for two years.

But during this time my knowledge of God deepened. I began to keep the Sabbath and attended church so regularly that many people thought I was a member. I continued to investigate the doctrines for myself, reading every Adventist book I could find. One of these was *The Great Controversy*. The book completely changed my former socialist philosophy of history, which had been a major stumbling block.

The doctrine of the gift of prophecy manifested through Ellen G. White was one I found difficult to understand, especially because many of my Adventist friends did not seem clear about it either. Some maintained the *Testimonies* were valid only in the time when they were written. Others said that certain statements were inspired while others were not, leaving us free to pick and choose. But it was clear to me I couldn't be baptized until I understood and accepted this doctrine. Providence led someone to place a copy of the book *E. G. White, Prophet of Destiny* in my hands. After reading it and reflecting on it, my most difficult questions were resolved.

I was baptized on August 30, 1997.

My conversion brought out the expected hostile reaction from my former comrades. Some tried to explain it as a passing phase or an "ideological crisis." Others reacted with hostility. But "if God be for us, who can be against us?" (Rom. 8:31). One of my former comrades, in witnessing my experience, rediscovered his own faith, and although he later died of a painful illness, before his death he fully accepted our hope in the promise of the resurrection.

When I enrolled once more at the university, instead of being the leader of a left-wing organization, I was elected president of the Adventist Student Center. After graduating, I served as legal advisor to ADRA Peru and law professor at the Peruvian Adventist University. I also worked as a freelance litigator for religious liberty issues, and I am considered a Peruvian scholar on church–state issues.

Most important of all, I rejoice in my friendship with Jesus, and together with my brothers and sisters I fight the good fight of faith while looking forward to the glorious return of our Lord.

---

* Translated into English with the title *Jesus Hypotheses* (n.p.: St. Paul Publications, 1977).

After completing his law studies, Marco Antonio Huaco received a master's degree in social sciences of religion at San Marcos University and later a master's degree in international human rights law at Strasbourg University in France. He is currently a legal and political advisor for the congress of the republic of Peru. E-mail: marcohuaco@gmail.com

Chapter 6

Two Cents and Half a Cabbage

· · · · · · · · ·

Leslie Kay

The Okanagan Valley, in the state of Washington, had put on a yellow and scarlet dress in the month of October, and although the days were warm and pleasant, the nights had become a torment to Leslie. The scraps of cardboard she placed in her sleeping bag every night had become less and less effective in warding off the cold. Nevertheless, there didn't seem to be any other solution. To buy another bag or more clothing was impossible. She had literally two cents in her pocket.

If only the money Barbara had promised would come, then maybe she could buy another bag and leave this beautiful but cold country for warmer climes in the south.

It had been 10 days since she had called Barbara in Los Angeles to tell her about her plight. But now she realized sadly that when she had called, her brain had been so foggy from the effects of marijuana that she could not remember even the postal code of the place. If a check *was* on its way, it was hardly possible to hope that it would arrive at its destination.

Today, as she had done many times before, Leslie stood on the side of the highway hoping that someone would give her a ride to the nearest post office in Tonasket, which was 45 miles from her campsite. While on the way, she attempted to convince herself that this would be the day the check would finally arrive. But once again she was disappointed. Seeing her hopeful face, the postmaster just shook his head and shrugged.

Leslie sighed deeply. There was nothing left for her now but to return to her "home," where she could look forward to half a cabbage and another cold night.

Walking backward down Highway 97 with her attention fixed on the oncoming traffic, the young hitchhiker reflected on her life. She realized she was tired. Not physically fatigued, but inwardly aching and exhausted. Empty.

She had left family and friends three years ago at age 20 to escape the emptiness that permeated her world and the lives of those she loved. She imagined it was contagious, indigenous to the environment. She convinced herself that if she fled far enough away, it couldn't catch her. She hadn't known that the virus of emptiness was within her, imprinted on her very self. Now—three years and some 20,000 restless miles later—she just wished her weary self would get lost.

All the propaganda had seemed believable: that LSD could "expand her consciousness," that studying the occult would develop her psychic powers, that Yoga could give her inner peace, and that getting in touch with the "god within" would enable her to transcend this meaningless material plane of existence. Yet here she stood, having learned a little about a lot that was irrelevant and staggering at her basic ignorance of anything that really mattered.

The gravel crunched as a white truck pulled over. She jogged up to it and cast a practiced eye on the driver. He was a man in his mid-30s with a neatly trimmed beard, glasses, and suspenders. His young son sat beside him, likewise in suspenders and long sleeves despite the warm day. *Church types*, she thought. Deciding they were harmless, she joined the driver and his son in the cab.

The boy smiled shyly as he looked up into her eyes and said, "Hi, my name's David. What's yours?"

His friendliness disarmed her habitual cynicism, and she returned his smile as she introduced herself. A lively conversation ensued, during which Ron identified himself and his son as Christians.

She knew she should feel uncomfortable with these people, but the truth was that she felt right at home. Where were the disapproving glances or the implied condemnation she had expected? All she felt in their presence was an affectionate concern and a refreshing earnestness and simplicity.

When Ron discovered his passenger was in a financial bind, he immediately invited her to stay at his little farm with his family of four for as long as she liked. He said his wife cooked wonderful vegetarian food, and they would be delighted to have her.

Naturally, she struggled with this invitation. What if these people were, at worst, some type of social deviants or bizarre cultists or, at best, propagandizing evangelists? What was their ulterior motive for wanting to help a stranger?

On the other hand, they obviously knew something she didn't. They were happy, and she was not. She wanted to know the source for their happiness, and admittedly, she was a very hungry vegetarian. She decided to accept their invitation.

For two weeks she stayed with that kind family. They shared their home and their food, as well as their six days of labor and seventh day of rest. They shared their prayers with her at every delicious meal and at morning and evening worship. Most of all, they shared their Lord with her—never aggressively but always attractively by the persuasive example of their family life. Their love was so contagious she fell in love with them.

Although they never pressed, the family made a direct knowledge of their God available to Leslie through Bibles and Christian books. One day when she was sure no one was looking, she picked up one of these books, intending only a casual perusal of the first chapter. But her attention became immediately riveted on the unfolding of a powerful drama, the focus of which was Christ on the Mount of Olives a few days before His crucifixion. His tears were not for Himself but for the inhabitants of Jerusalem—the objects of His unrequited love.

"Divine pity, yearning love, found utterance in the mournful words: 'O Jerusalem, Jerusalem, thou that killest the prophets, and stonest them which are sent unto thee, how often would I have gathered thy children together, even as a hen gathereth her chickens under her wings, and ye would not!'" *(The Great Controversy,* p. 21).

She was stricken by the pathos of the scene. Here was the Creator making Himself vulnerable to His creation—concerning Himself more with the fate of His rejecters than with Himself. He yearned to be their Savior but refused to press Himself upon them against their will.

From some dark subterranean chamber she did not know existed, a great sob rose up as though its anchor had been severed at last. She knew without question that in some mysterious way she, too, had been rejecting truth and had been a participant in the crucifixion of this Holy Being. As her soul was laid bare within her, the weight of her guilt and rebellion would surely have smothered her had not that awful sob pleaded wordlessly for cleansing and fellowship.

How could she have thought, all this time, that she had been devotedly pursuing God? She had been pursuing some god, perhaps, but not this One. While she had been determinedly evading Him, this God had been relentlessly pursuing her soul, gathering her to Himself and waiting for her consent.

In the quiet of that godly home, she heard His invitation clearly: "Come to the wedding banquet. I have made everything ready. Leave the crumbs and scraps of your old life behind. I am the Bread of Life. I am waiting for you."

Drawn by the love in His voice, she determined not to disappoint Him any longer but, by His grace, to accept.

Chapter 7

Never Alone

Álvaro Martínez

Iwas born in the south of Mexico in a little village near the town of
Tlalchapa, in the state of Guerrero.

When I was 5 years old, my parents separated because my father was
an alcoholic and irresponsible. My mother was left with five small children
and no way to support us, so she left us with my grandmother while she
went north to explore the possibility of getting us into the United States.
Before long she returned and took us with her.

While on that first exploratory journey, my mother converted to the
Pentecostal religion, and when we got to the border, we stayed with a
woman named Carmela Hernández, who belonged to the same faith.

First we tried to cross with my mother's brother, but we were stopped
at a police checkpoint and turned back. Then my mother contracted some
"coyotes" to take us across, but they said I could not go because I was too
little. My older brothers and sisters were big enough to run if they were in
danger of being caught, but I was only 5 and would get everyone in trouble.
Señora Carmela said she would take care of me, so the rest of the family
went on, and I was left behind.

After my mother left, I didn't hear from her again for a year. I remember
how much I longed for her. At night I would go out and look around. I
could see thousands of lights, and I thought that behind one of those lights
must be my mother. I saw the airplanes overhead, and I asked them to
bring my mother. I was very sad.

My situation was even more miserable because Señora Carmela beat
me a lot, something my mother never did. She had a thick lash made of
leather, and I was very much afraid of her. Every morning I had to get up
early to empty the slop jars, sweep and mop the floor, and make the beds
before I could go to school. Señora Carmela had a daughter about my age
who never seemed to have anything to do.

Near the Pentecostal church there was a woman who had a children's home, and one day I heard her say to Señora Carmela, "Let me have the boy. I'll take care of him."

But she replied, "No, his mother gave him to me. He's mine now, and I'm going to keep him." When I heard that, I felt terrible. My own mother had given me away!

But as the months went by, a feeling of indifference began to replace the pain. One afternoon I was playing when I heard someone come and ask for Señora Carmela. Her older daughter said, "She's not here. Who is looking for her?"

"I am Maximina Jaimes, Álvaro's mother."

I heard her voice, but I didn't feel any desire to run and embrace her. I peeked around the corner to see her, but I had completely lost any feeling for my mother.

When she saw me in the doorway, she held out her arms and said, "I am your mother, son." But I just stood there. She came over and hugged me, and then she sat down and began to chat with Carmela's daughter while I continued to play.

After Señora Carmela came back, old memories and feelings began to stir in my heart. I went over and stood by my mother, and she began to caress me, but when I glanced at Señora Carmela, she was frowning. She tossed her head a little, indicating that she wanted me to get out of there. I obeyed quickly.

Several days went by while my mother tried to find a way to take me with her, and I began to feel love for her once again. The way she treated me was so different.

One day Mother took me to visit her brother who lived in Tijuana. He was the same uncle who first tried to help us cross the border. He and his wife were living in a new part of the city, and their house had no water or electricity. After our visit we boarded a bus to return to Señora Carmela's house. As we rode along Mother told me that she had tried very hard but could find no way to take me with her. She then asked whether I wanted to stay with Señora Carmela or with my uncle. Without hesitation I said, "With my uncle." I did not want to stay with Señora Carmela because I was afraid of her.

I remember the last time I saw my mother. It was early in the morning and still dark. She did not realize I was awake. She kissed me gently on my forehead and said to my uncle's wife, "Well, I'm leaving him with you. I'll be sending you money, so please take care of him. I'll try to come again before long and get him."

As I heard those words, I pulled the sheet over my face and began to cry desperately. I don't know why I didn't cling to her feet and try to stop her from going. I recall only that I cried and cried. I cried a lot that time.

About two weeks later another uncle stopped on his way to Guerrero, and he said to me, "What are you doing here? Come with me, and I'll take you back to where you were born. That's where your grandparents are. You'll be better off there." So he convinced me, and I went with him.

Back in my hometown I stayed for a time with my uncle and later with my grandmother. I enjoyed school, but home life was miserable because my grandmother's husband was very fierce and hot-tempered. At 9 years old I had to take an ax and a machete and go out to bring in a load of firewood like a man. If I brought in scraps or small pieces, he would beat me. He would yell at me that I was not a girl and must not act like one. Even the most insignificant thing could make him angry. I have many scars because he would beat me with whatever he could find at hand—his machete, a piece of firewood, or whatever.

One time we went into the hills to look for fence posts. We were trying to break a young donkey, and every time we would put anything on its back, it would take off running. The old man ordered me to catch it and get on its back, which was no easy task because it had no bridle or saddle, just a rope around its neck. I was able to catch the animal, but when I tried to get up, it would jump and run again.

The old man swore at me and said I was useless and no good. Then he tried it, and the donkey bucked and kicked and threw him off. He landed hard on his backside. At that he was even more furious, and he began to beat me with the broad side of his machete. I put my hands in back to defend myself, and the machete cut my hand. It was a long time before the wound healed, and I still have a scar from it. My grandmother scolded him for what he had done, but that was all. And he continued to be very angry with me over the incident.

How I longed for my mother! I felt hopeless and desperate, and about two weeks later I could stand it no longer. One afternoon when they had gone to town, I laid a shirt on the bed and placed three or four changes of clothing on it. I tied these up in a bundle and went to live on the streets of Tlalchapa, which was about two miles from the village where I was born.

My grandmother came looking for me several times. Once she even brought two policemen and took me back to her house, but I was not happy there. I would just cry and cry and then go back to live on the streets again.

After sleeping on the streets and drifting around for some time, I went to see an Adventist woman who ran a public telephone service. In those days there were no cell phones, and only a few individuals had phones at home. So people would call for their friends or relatives at the public telephone office, and a messenger would go and tell them to come to the office and wait for the people to call them back. This woman gave me work as a messenger.

Every morning I would walk the two miles back to the village where I was born and go to school. As soon as classes were over, I would hurry back to Tlalchapa and work all afternoon and evening at the telephone office. This kind woman also gave me lunch and supper and a place to sleep.

Several years passed. Then one day when the woman who owned the phone service was not there, Lucila, her secretary, asked me take a message to a place that was very far away. I told her I had no bicycle, and it was too far to walk. She said, "I don't know how you're going to do it, but that message has to get there right away."

On the days when I had no classes, I would often help the owner's son milk cows. He had a four-wheeler, and I would ride with him on the back. I had always been good at looking at something and figuring out how it works, so I decided to take the four-wheeler to deliver the message.

When the woman came back, her secretary told her I had taken the four-wheeler. She became very upset and fired me on the spot. It was about 11:00 p.m. I went outside and sat on the curb. A little while later the secretary came out and asked me where I was going to stay.

"I don't know," I said. "I'll figure something out."

"Well, why don't you come to my house," she said.

"No," I replied. "I'll just stay here on the street. It's not the first time."

But she continued to insist, so I went with her. Her mother sold chickens and her father baked bread, and I began to help them while continuing in school. Lucila got me a bicycle so I did not have to walk the two miles to my village for classes. I stayed with them for some time.

Portable cassette players were starting to be popular then, and I began to dream about how wonderful it would be if I could listen to music on the way to school and back. The government had started to give me a scholarship of 450 pesos a month. One day, just before the time of month when I was to receive this money, Lucila sent me to the pharmacy with 200 pesos to buy some medicine. When I got back, I gave her the pills, and she said, "Just put the change on top of the wardrobe." I foolishly decided to take 150 pesos to buy myself a cassette player. I thought she wouldn't notice, and I planned to pay her back when my scholarship money arrived. But that night she counted the money and discovered that some of it was missing.

At first I tried to deny what I had done, but when she began to talk about calling the police, I told her I had borrowed the money and was intending to return it as soon as I got my scholarship. After scolding me a lot, she said she would give me another chance. I stayed a few more days after that, but everyone in the house seemed to be angry with me, and they blamed me for everything that went wrong. So I left and began sleeping in an abandoned house that consisted of just some crumbling old walls without a roof. My only possession of any value was my new cassette player. Before long, someone stole it from the ruins. It was the only thing I had of any value, and someone took it.

Sometime later I met a boy who said to me, "Why don't you ask for help from Señora Herminia Alarcón? She is the president of the DIF [a family service agency run by the government]. Just tell her you don't have any place to stay. Maybe she will help you."

He even offered to go with me to talk with her.

"What about your family?" Señora Herminia asked. "Can't your grandmother help you?" I told her a little bit about my situation.

She looked pensive. "Well, come by my house around 5:00 p.m.," she said. "My husband isn't home right now. But we'll talk it over and see what we can do for you."

When I arrived at the appointed time, he hadn't come yet, but she said, "Where are your things?"

"Ah, . . . well, I didn't bring them."

"Go get them and come back," she said.

I did as I was told, and upon my return she showed me to a room in the house. Her husband, Don Francisco Alarcón, was the mayor of Tlalchapa, and he came in fairly late. I happened to be passing through the hallway as they were talking, and I overheard him say, "No way! That's the boy who stole from Lucila." (Lucila, by that time, was his secretary.) "If he stole from Lucy, what makes you think he won't steal from us? You'll have to figure out what to do with him, but I definitely don't want him around here." When I heard that, my hopes fell.

Then I heard Señora Herminia say, "Well, all right, we'll just let him stay this week, and you can see what you think."

"Hummph!" he grumbled. "It'll be at your risk."

The next morning I woke up early to water the plants and sweep and clean the courtyard. I tried to anticipate their needs and be as helpful as possible. Don Franciso was organizing a big fiesta and fandango at his house, and I worked hard to help him get set up, and then I operated the sound system. I tried to make myself indispensable. At the end of the first week they didn't say anything about my leaving, and I stayed on.

Señora Herminia encouraged me to study, and she got my records transferred to Tlalchapa so I didn't have to go to my village every day to study. I continued to do well in school, and I was eating better and feeling happier than at any time in my life. In 1996 I entered a sand drawing competition, and I won first place in our area. So the señora took me all the way to Acapulco to compete there. The truth is they were very kind to me. Altogether I was with them three years, and I became very fond of them.

But when I was in the sixth grade, my school friends began to pressure me to go out at night. "No," I would tell them. "I have to study. Señora Herminia won't let me go out."

They would say, "What? She's not even your mother. She's holding you back too much. She's treating you like a baby." Their words swayed me, and I began to think I needed more freedom.

One day Señora Herminia sent me to town for something, and instead of coming right back, I went to a place that had video games. I started playing and lost track of time. When I finally came home, it was very late. Señora Herminia was waiting for me behind the door, and as soon as I came in, she lashed me across the back with a belt. By that time I was 13 years old. Nobody had hit me for a long time, and I became raging mad. I cursed at her and said, "I'm tired of being here. You don't give me any freedom."

All night I nursed my anger, and the next morning I told her, "I'm leaving."

"Well," she said, "If you're tired of us, then go."

Still, I stayed on a few more days. Actually, I was reluctant to leave, but was too proud to admit it and too stubborn to change my mind. When I said goodbye to Don Francisco, both of us had tears in our eyes.

"Where are you going?" he asked me.

"Some friends have invited me to say at their house," I told him.

That was true, but the friends were not home at the time. They had left for the United States several months earlier. I went to their house anyway and slept under a staircase. I would go to the market every morning to earn a few pesos for something to eat and then go to school in the afternoon.

I was finishing sixth grade, which is the end of elementary school, and because of my grades I had earned third place in the honor guard for the graduation ceremony. But in the end I did not march in the honor guard and did not attend the ceremony, because I was overwhelmed by the fact that all of my classmates would be going with their parents or family members and that I would be all alone.

On graduation night I went to the school and stood in a place where I could see everything. I watched the honor guard go by, but I was not in it. I looked through the window and saw the graduates sitting there, but my place was empty. Then I heard them read the names, and nobody responded for me. I was very sad.

I slept under the staircase for some time. Then the people came home and said they didn't want me there any longer, so I went back to the street. At times I would sleep in the kiosk in the central plaza. At other times I would sleep on the seat of an old car.

Later I went to see my mother's sister who lived in Tlalchapa. She had seven children, but I hoped she would let me stay with her, and she did. About that time I started working at a brickyard collecting broken pieces. I could earn 20 or 30 pesos a day there, which I brought home to my aunt.

One day when I came home from work, my aunt said a man had stopped by looking for someone to take care of his goats. "Well, I already have a job at the brick factory," I told her.

"Yes, but he's my cousin," she said. "He needs a boy, and I told him you would do it. He will pay you 800 pesos a month and give you lunch early so that you can go to school."

So I started working for Don Salomón Machuca. I was happy because he promised I could have Saturdays free. I belonged to a city-league soccer team, and we practiced on Saturday. But after a few weeks Don Salomón told me he needed me every day, so the soccer had to go. He had promised to pay me 800 pesos a month, but he paid me only 500. However, I did enjoy my work and was doing well. It wasn't easy to find part-time work in Tlalchapa, so I stayed.

After I had been there a while, the Machucas' older sons, who were working in the United States, came home for a visit. I got along well with the boys, and one of them was especially kind to me. He gave me some lotion and a change of clothing. I was really happy because I had never had good clothes like that. But when Señora Machuca saw me washing the clothes, she took them away, saying, "These belong to my son."

"But he gave them to me," I protested.

"Of course not," she said. "When did you ever have nice clothes like that?" And she took them.

By this time a new school year was about to start, and I was supposed to enter middle school. But when I went to enroll, the principal said I had to bring a parent or a sponsor to sign for me. I asked my aunt, but she said she already had seven children and couldn't help.

I asked my employer, Don Salomón, and he said, "Sure, I'll be your sponsor." But when the time came, he said, "What do you want to go to school for, anyway? You see my sons? They didn't study. They went to the United States, and look at all they have."

"OK," I said, but I was not happy.

I went to speak with the principal, and I told him, "I'll be responsible for myself. I always was in elementary school. I paid my own expenses. If any supplies or school fees were needed, I always bought them."

"How old are you?" he asked, eyeing me suspiciously.

"Fifteen."

"That's too old," he replied. "You can't enroll."

Several of my classmates were the same age or older. But for some reason he had decided not to let me continue. Finally he said, "If you really want to study, go and enroll in the open study plan for adults."

At that point my pride took over, and I said, "Never mind. I'll go the United States instead."

Don Salomón had told me a number of times, "When my boys go back to the States, you can go with them, and you can make a lot of money there."

The day finally came when the boys left to go back. I kept expecting Don Salomón to follow up on what he had said, but it didn't happen. He never said a word. They went, and I was left behind.

So after thinking it over for a while, I decided to enroll in the open study plan for middle school. The man in charge was friendly and helpful. He gave me the books and study guides, and I went in once a month for the exams.

When I finished all the requirements, he gave me a middle school certificate, but he said, "Be sure you get good grades in senior high. I don't want anyone saying I gave you the certificate without your deserving it."

After some time Don Salomón sold the goats and bought some cows. I became good at milking and continued working for 500 pesos a month. Don Salomón's younger sons, who were still at home, loved going to races and parties. They would often leave me to take care of the animals because they knew they could count on me. During this time I began to think about Don Juan Rodriguez, my grandmother's husband. I realized he had taught me a lot about hard work and responsibility. I knew how to build a fence, set posts in line, and do many other things thanks to his instruction. He was very harsh, and I resented that aspect, but I was grateful for the practical skills I had learned from him.

Don Pedro was a nearby neighbor who watched me pass by at the same time every morning to deliver the milk. One day he was waiting for me. "Hello," he said, "I see you are working for Don Salomón."

"Yes," I said. "I help take care of his cows."

"Do you think you'll keep on working for him in the future?"

"As long as he keeps paying me, yes."

"And how much does he pay you?" the man wanted to know.

"Ah, well . . . 500 pesos a month."

"No way!" he said. "The man is exploiting you."

"No, it's OK," I told him. "He also gives me room and board."

"Even so," he insisted. "Look, I'll make you an offer. I have a little farm at the edge of town, and I need someone to take care of it. I've seen how you go by every day at the same time, and I know you are responsible. I will pay you 1,000 pesos. I just want you to live there. In the morning I go over to milk. Of course, you will help me with that and take care of the calves. In the afternoon you can go to school."

The idea seemed like a good one; after all, there was nothing wrong with earning 1,000 pesos. In senior high I would have to pay tuition and buy uniforms and new shoes.

So a few days later I spoke with Don Salomón. It was early in the morning, and we were milking. I said to him, "I guess I won't be working for you anymore."

"Why not?" he wanted to know.

"Well, I've been offered another job, and it pays more."

"How much are they offering you?"

"A thousand pesos," I told him.

He was silent for a while; then he said, "All right. That's better for you, so you better take it."

About three days before the end of the month, he said, "Look, Álvaro, I've really gotten fond of you. I'm going to increase your wages to 800 a month so you will be content and stay with me."

Well, in truth, I was fond of him, too, and their house was very close to the senior high school. So I said, "All right, I'll stay."

But when the end of the month came, Don Salomón said that 800 pesos was too much. He couldn't pay me that much after all. "I'll pay you 600 if you agree, and if not, feel free to go and work for Don Pedro."

By that time it was too late. Someone else had taken the job with Don Pedro, and I didn't know of any other place to get part-time work, so I stayed, and he paid me 600 pesos a month.

Not long after that, Don Salomón sold a good portion of his cows, and he said to me, "Look, we're not going to be able to pay you anymore. Go ahead and see where you can find work; we will at least give you food and let you stay here."

I looked but could find no work that would let me continue in school, so I stayed. I still got up early and helped the family just as I always had. And once in a while they would give me 20 pesos. Don Salomón had promised me food, but when I would go in to eat, Señora Machuca always seemed irritated to see me there, so I often didn't eat or would go to the market to find something rather than face her.

Toward the end of my final year of high school, someone put up posters announcing a series of bullfights in a nearby stadium. Several of my school friends wanted to go. Don Salomón had a Nissan pickup, so I asked him, "Could you lend me your pickup?"

He said, "Yes, just be sure you put some gas in it."

"OK, I'll do that," I promised.

"When do you need it?"

"Tomorrow evening. Some friends and I want to see the bullfights."

"OK, sure, no problem," he said. So I went to wash it and get it ready.

The next afternoon, October 17, 2003, five or six classmates and I went to the fights. While there we started to drink. Pretty soon we returned to Tlalchapa and drank some more. About 11:00 p.m. we decided to go back to the bullring again. I was driving, and we were all pretty drunk by that time. We were racing along this narrow dirt road when suddenly we were blinded by headlights of a car that was coming straight toward us. I swerved to the right. The pickup bounced wildly over a ditch and turned on its side.

Before long the police arrived. "What happened?" they asked.

I told them.

"Was anyone hurt?

"No, we're all OK." It seemed like a miracle that none of us was hurt. They looked around, checked everything, and then let us go.

But we had knocked over some fence posts. So at 6:00 the next morning I went back to fix the fence because there were crops in the field.

Around 7:00 I was just finishing the repair job when I saw a police car pull up. The officer strolled over and asked me my name. When I identified myself, he said, "OK, get in the car."

Alarmed, I asked what was the matter.

"It seems you killed someone last night," he said.

Now I was really terrified. "What do you mean? You were here, and you saw we were all OK."

He didn't answer. When we got to the station, they told me that about 80 or 100 yards from where we had flipped over, on the opposite side of the road, about 1:00 to 2:00 in the morning someone had found the body of a young woman.

A few minutes later a man came in and pointed at me and said, "Yes, that's him. He's the one who killed my sister."

It turned out that two people were coming from the bullfights on their bicycles, and the car that ran us off the road was also coming from that same direction. The two bicycles and the other vehicle had veered off the road, just as we had, to avoid a head-on collision.

If someone had died, I didn't see how they could know for sure who was responsible. But the young man made out an affidavit stating that he had seen me and identified me at the scene of the accident. He said he had asked me why I was driving crazy like that.

Terrified and confused, I desperately tried to defend myself. Finally we each gave a sworn statement to the police, giving our position.

Then I was arrested and handcuffed. "You are going to prison," they told me, "because you did it."

At that point I began to cry out of sheer frustration and anguish. The judicial police came and began to threaten me, telling me in foul language what they were going to do to make me tell the truth. I spent that night handcuffed to an antenna and sitting on a barrel of gasoline. Before morning I was shivering from the cold, sick to my stomach and dizzy from breathing the gasoline vapor.

About 8:00 they took me to the prison in Coyuca de Catalán and put me in a holding cell. That is where they keep people for 72 hours until they are formally charged. This also gives someone time to post bail for them.

About 10:00 or 10:30 in the morning I saw Don Salomón come into the building with his sons. I was very happy. *They are coming to help me,* I thought. But no, they were coming to make things worse. Don Salomón swore out an affidavit stating that I had stolen his pickup, that I had taken it without his knowledge or consent, and that there were parts missing.

Later a doctor who had been my teacher came in to see me. "There's nothing I can do to help you," he said. But he went and told my father, and my father brought me a little rolled-up mattress. That was the only time I saw him. We never spoke before or after that, but he brought me a mattress, and I was grateful.

That first night in the holding cell I didn't sleep at all. I spent the night in despair and bitterness of soul. I cried and cursed everyone and everything that came to mind—I cursed God, my parents, the day I was born, the police, and the justice system. I remembered all the problems and troubles I had gone through. I had worked so hard and sacrificed to at least finish high school. Now that dream was gone too. I thought of all that and continued to weep.

After 72 hours they took me out of the holding cell and officially consigned me to prison. They said I had nine months to prove my innocence. But how was I going to do that? I didn't have a clue. The man swore he had seen me and spoken to me. He said that I had done it. It was impossible for me to defend myself from inside the prison, and who was going to help me?

The government assigned me a defense attorney, but as is always the case, she was also representing many others. Unfortunately, in our country everything depends on money. Although these lawyers are paid by the state, your family has to give them money as well. Otherwise your case can be held up indefinitely.

The guards led me into the prison and set me to washing dishes. Other prisoners crowded around asking, "What did you do? What are you in for?" They began to shove and to try to order me around. "Go get this!" "Do this," they said, all the while cursing and threatening me.

At that point a man from Tlalchapa came in. Someone told him that the newcomer was from his hometown. Knowing what I was facing, he came to my defense. "Wow! It's great to see you, man!" he said loudly as if he knew me. "He's from my hometown. Leave him alone, will you?" he said to the crowd.

Because of the respect they had for this man, they backed off. Then he said, "Come on with me, man. We'll do a lot of things together." He taught me how to cope. He was an expert at making belts out of hemp and leather, and he taught me these things. I really owe him a lot.

About 3:00 in the afternoon on that first day in prison, a Pentecostal lay preacher who had just finished conducting a meeting saw me and came right over, "Don't worry," he told me. "God has a plan for your life."

I felt a great rage well up in my soul. "Don't talk to me about God!" I replied. "I don't believe in God."

"Don't be like that," he said.

"If there was a God, my parents wouldn't be separated. If there was a God, I wouldn't have suffered hunger, cold, and betrayal. I wouldn't be all alone in life, and I wouldn't be here now. Excuse me, but there is no God; don't talk to me about God. Go away, please."

This man came every Friday to hold services, and he would single me out and try to talk, but I would hide from him. He usually got there at 2:00 p.m.

and left about 3:00, which was when they fed us. Sometimes I would forget, and then he would greet me warmly, and I would think, *Oh no, not again.*

"How's it going, buddy?" he would say. "How've you been?" Then he would try to talk to me about God and invite me to attend his meetings.

"I've got to go now. It's time to eat," I usually said. Once or twice I did go to his meetings, but I took no real interest in them.

Time went on, and I waited for my attorney to help me. She would come and talk with the other prisoners she was helping, but she always ignored me. Maybe their relatives were paying her; I don't know. But when I approached her, she would always say, "Look, Álvaro, I haven't had a chance to check your records; I'll let you know."

They had given me nine months to resolve the case and bring it to court. When the time was up, my lawyer asked for a one-month extension, then another, and another. After a full year she looked for me one day and said, "Álvaro, I have news for you. I have read your document file."

"What does it say?" I asked her.

"Do you have money to put up for a bail bond?" she asked.

"Where am I going to get money for bail? No, of course I don't."

"It's pretty high," she said. "You need to put up 137,700 pesos." That would have been the equivalent of US$20,000.

"They shouldn't have wasted their time," I told her.

"But at least there's hope. What about your family? Can they help?" Then she added, "Another good thing is that the man who is accusing you seems to contradict himself a lot. What we need to do is to get some proof that you are innocent."

"How can we do that?"

"First, we need to have a face-to-face meeting with this fellow in front of the judge. I'll let you know when we can arrange it."

Before long I received an official notification of a meeting with my accuser. I expected the attorney to say, "Look, you need to say thus and so. Here is how you're going to defend yourself," but it never happened. In fact, she didn't even show up at the hearing. The government attorney was there. It was his job to take the side of the accuser and make me look as guilty as possible.

First they read the affidavit given by the young man. Then he reaffirmed it, saying, "Yes, I saw him. He got out of the pickup, and I went personally and spoke with him and asked him why he was driving like that."

It was a total lie, and of course, I said that his statement was not true. "You weren't even there when the police came."

But he continued to swear that he was there and that he saw me. The state attorney defended him. There was no one to defend me, and I didn't know what to do.

After a while another lawyer who was passing by said, "Where's your attorney?"

I said, "She didn't come."

He said to the judge, "This boy can't be here making statements without a lawyer." That was the end of the hearing.

I went out of there totally discouraged because my accuser had said things that had not happened, and they had believed him.

When I got back, my cellmate said, "How did it go, buddy?"

"Really bad," I told him. "This fellow is making up stuff, and they believe him." I told him what had happened.

He had a lot more experience than I did, and he asked me, "Don't you have a lawyer?"

"She didn't even show up," I told him.

"When that happens, don't even open your mouth. You have a right to be silent. And in regard to this boy, I don't know if you were guilty or not. But if it's like you say, next time you have to defend yourself."

"But what if I say something wrong and get in worse trouble?" I asked.

"If you play it straight and tell the truth, you'll come out all right. Let me give you an example. He says that he recognized you and that he came up and spoke to you personally. You can say to him, 'If you really saw me, I want you to identify me. What color of jacket was I wearing, and what kind of a cap did I have on?'"

The fact is that I was not wearing any cap or jacket, just a striped shirt. "That sounds good," I told him.

I thought there would be another hearing soon, but time continued to go by. The attorney who supposedly was helping me never came again. She took a job somewhere else, and three more years went by. I seemed to be totally forgotten in the prison system.

After about two years I started to more or less believe in God, and I began to go to services with the Pentecostals. At the end of the third year another man I knew from Tlalchapa, an Adventist, came to the same prison under false charges. Every morning we would see him praying. Then as soon as they opened the cells and let us out into the yard, he would walk around with his Bible and talk to us about God. A lot of people made fun of him and thought he was crazy.

Because of this man, Brother Malaquías, members of the Adventist church started to come to the prison. First it was just visitors who came to see him. Nearly everyone in Tlalchapa knew me, and a lot of the visitors who came to see him would greet me. Sometimes they would bring me a bar of soap or other personal items. Other times they would tell me that someone had asked about me or sent me greetings. After that I didn't feel quite so forgotten or alone.

Pretty soon the Adventists started to hold meetings every Saturday at 4:00 p.m., and Brother Malaquías would invite us to attend. "Sure, I'll go in a minute," I would tell him.

I never went, but I usually sat nearby in case anyone from Tlalchapa sent something for me, which they often did.

I was working at the time making leather belts with a friend named José Alfredo. One day we were completely out of soap and other personal items, so I said to him, "Today let's see if the Adventists invite us to their meeting. Maybe they'll hand out some gifts at the end." So we sat near the entrance of the meeting place hoping for an invitation, but to our surprise, this time they just passed us by and went on in. We were sitting there, feeling disappointed, when a woman who came in late walked right over to where we were sitting and invited us.

"Sure," I said, as I always did, "we'll be right there." But I nudged José Alfredo and said to him, "This time we're really going."

Instead of the shouting and excitement I was used to at the Pentecostal meetings, the preacher made a simple and quiet presentation—so quiet, in fact, that I fell asleep. I woke up just in time to hear him say, "When you feel that you've lost everything, when you feel everyone has turned their back on you, even people you never thought would betray you, remember, there is Someone who will never leave you. That is Jesus. When you feel alone and discouraged, go to Him in faith and with your heart surrender to His will. He is the only one who can give you peace."

When the meeting was over, I took the soap and other gifts and left. I had not attended because I wanted to hear the message, but after that I never missed another meeting.

Sometime later the Adventist group decided to hold an evangelistic series. Some of the folks who came to these meetings from Tlalchapa were people I cared a lot about. One of them was the woman I had worked for as a messenger boy. She came with her children. I was very happy to see them, and they brought me clothing and other things.

The preacher in this series was a young minister named Abimael

Vázquez. He talked to us about the Sabbath, baptism, and other subjects. On Wednesday he said to me, "I need to talk with you alone after the meeting. Can you stay for a little while?"

He invited me to make a decision for Christ. "I like your message," I told him, "but I don't feel ready to be baptized. I am afraid."

He said to me, "Look, Álvaro, I don't know why you are here, and I don't know what you have gone through. What I do know is that God has a plan for your life. This week He wants you to become part of His family. He wants you to come to the arms of Jesus. He is going to do something special for you."

I had been sick for a long time with a chronic skin condition. Instead of getting better, it was steadily getting worse. The doctors said I would just have to live with it. That week it was especially bad, and I was miserable and discouraged. Then I remembered what the pastor had said at the first meeting I had attended. He had said that when you feel everyone and everything is against you, go to Jesus, because He has never turned His back on anyone.

On Friday evening I went to my cell and, for the first time ever, knelt down and prayed. "It's hard for me to believe in You, Lord," I said, "because I can't see You, but I've heard that You have done a lot of miracles. They've told me that blessed are those who believe in You. You know my situation."

I got up from my knees feeling totally at peace. I was no longer worried about whether I was sick or not. I read a verse from the Bible, and then I lay down and slept peacefully.

The next morning, Sabbath morning, I got up and went to take a shower. To my amazement, my skin was as clean and normal as if I had never had a problem. God had heard my prayer and healed me! That was six years ago, and to this day it has never come back.

At the meeting that morning, just before the baptismal service, the pastor made another call. I was standing toward the rear hanging on to a table. In spite of the wonderful miracle God had done for me, I held on to that table because I was afraid. A powerful force was drawing me forward, but I held back. A war raged within my soul. The pastor said, "The candidates are ready, and we are going to proceed with the baptism, but I want to extend one more invitation. God is waiting for one more soul to surrender."

One of my friends signaled that he would go forward if I went, but I put my head down and looked away, still clinging to the table. Some minutes went by. Finally the pastor said, "Well, it seems no one else is going to respond, but I don't want to pray without making a special appeal to one young man whom I am sure God is calling. I am sure God has performed a miracle in his life, and he wants to surrender to Jesus. That young man is you, Álvaro. Come. Jesus is calling you."

When he mentioned my name, tears began to fall from my eyes, and I let go of the table. Then he said once more, "Come to Jesus. He has wonderful things in store for you."

I was the last one. Eight of us were baptized that day. I don't know where the others are now, but for me it was the beginning of a marvelous new chapter in my life.

Not long after that Sister Marisela, an Adventist member from Tlalchapa, asked me about my case. Then she spoke with a judge who had recently been appointed to the court, and before long another hearing was scheduled. After four years in prison and three years after the first hearing, I was to have another chance to defend myself.

This time I remembered the words of my cellmate. So I said to the young man who was accusing me, "If you are sure you saw me and spoke to me, I want you to answer a question. If you answer correctly, I will accept that you are telling the truth, but if not, then everything you have said is really a lie. You say that you saw me. I need you to identify me more. Tell me what color jacket and cap I was wearing. That shouldn't be hard if you were close and spoke to me."

And he said, "The truth is I didn't really see you. I could tell it was you when I saw you from a distance, but it was dark." This contradicted directly what he had stated in his sworn affidavit.

At the conclusion of the hearing the judge spoke with Sister Marisela and said, "This boy shouldn't be here. He should be free. He's just here because he didn't have anyone to stand up for him. But at this point, there's no way I can declare him innocent. Why? Because he has been here four years without a sentence. If I declare him innocent, we will all be in trouble, because the higher court will say, 'Why did you keep him there four years if he was innocent?' I have just been appointed judge, and I can't take that risk. What I can do is give him the minimum sentence. What he needs to do is rest his case and wait for the sentence." So that is what I did. The maximum sentence, they told me, would be 12 years, and the minimum four.

The day for the sentencing finally came. I was at peace, completely prepared for whatever would happen. I felt no assurance that I would go free, but I knew God would be glorified.

They brought me in, and the judge said she had decided to give me eight years. I noticed she was looking at me curiously, evidently waiting to see my reaction. The secretary said, "Don't you have anything to say?"

"No," I replied.

Then she said, "That's strange. Most prisoners curse or threaten us when they hear their sentence."

I said, "This has been the best possible experience for me. If I were not here, I might be dead. And if I hadn't stayed this long, I would never have known how much God loves me. If He wants me to be here longer, He can bring some good out of it, and it will be for His glory. Just tell me where I need to sign."

When I went up to sign, the secretary said, "Álvaro, your sentence is not really eight years; it's four. And you have already served your time."

A week later they sent me to a prison in another city and told me I would be there 20 days while they processed the paperwork for my release. The truth is that those 20 days seemed like an eternity. At the end of that time they called a group of us who were being released and began to read our names one by one as they released each prisoner to the open arms of his family. They left me for last, because there was no one there for me.

I walked out the door of the prison and stood there looking around. True, no one was there to receive me, but unlike what had happened in the past, I now knew for sure that I was not alone and would never really be alone again.

Some friends from the local Adventist church helped me purchase a bus ticket back to Tlalchapa, and when I got there, Pastor Abimael Vázquez let me stay at his house until I could get established again.

While I was staying with the pastor, every day after work I would help him conduct meetings, give Bible studies, and visit and pray with people. Every day I was drawn more and more to the work he was doing, and I became convicted that God was calling me to ministry.

The story of how God opened the doors for me to study is another miracle. But I have now finished the first year of the ministerial course at the University of Navojoa.

Mine is an unfinished story of grace that continues to unfold every day. What the future holds I do not know, but of one thing I am sure: Through all the sad moments, all the twists and turns of my life, in spite of all my mistakes, God has been there for me, and in His own strange and mysterious way, He has turned these things into blessings for the honor and glory of His name.

Chapter 8

The Meaning of Life

. . . .

Ala and Elena Shuedova

Ala

Elena and I were born in L'viv, an industrial city in the Ukraine with a population of some 900,000.

Looking back on it now, I would say we had a happy childhood. True, we were poor and there were problems, but we were happy. In fact, I would say we had the kind of childhood you usually only read about in books. It was our mother who made it that way.

Mother is a talented woman. She has a warm personality and a lively sense of humor. She is Russian (not Ukrainian), and she managed to impart to us the idea that something special was expected of us as inheritors of the rich cultural tradition of the Russian people.

She was dedicated to her children and her home. She taught us how to work by having us work at her side from the time we were very small. She took time to play with us and always stressed the things she felt we needed to know to be proper young women. I remember many happy hours sitting by her side while the three of us made beautiful things with needle and thread.

Father was a shoemaker. Gentle and soft-spoken by nature, he loved us dearly, but his world was very different from ours. His concept of what was required of him as a true man kept him outside our circle most of the time. His life centered on his job and, after hours, on the billiard hall and card games and drinking with a group of friends.

Father would often sit us down for serious talks, even when we were quite small. "You must be wise and look out for yourselves," he would tell us solemnly. "Always be ready to defend yourselves from people who might try to take advantage of your innocence and good looks. And above all, you must use your heads to think and search for the meaning of life."

Father himself never seemed to find the meaning of life that he so often urged us to look for. As time went on, his frustration and unhappiness grew, and so did his drinking. Sometimes after a night of drinking he would come home in the early-morning hours and get us out of bed to listen while he gave us long, angry speeches. He would stride back and forth and loudly warn us to look out for evil men, and he never failed to add that we must look for the meaning of life. Often he would turn abusive and blame Mother for all his troubles. She would put her head down and weep in silence, because answering only made it worse.

By the time Elena and I were in high school, the situation at home had become very serious. Father was drinking more or less constantly, and he was often violent and abusive. In the Soviet Union the secondary program has heavy academic requirements. Day after day we would go to classes and sit for examinations while physically and emotionally exhausted after another night of Father's rampages.

As things got worse, Mother's family began to urge her to put Father out and ask for a divorce or a legal separation, but she would only weep and shake her head. Somehow she felt she really was to blame as Father always said, and that if she would only try harder, things would get better. But things did not get better; they soon became impossible.

One night I packed up all of Father's clothes and personal items and waited for him to come home. At 2:00 a.m. he staggered in, kicked the door, and began to shout and threaten us as usual. I brought out his things and set them on the floor. Father stopped shouting and stared at me. "Take your things and go," I told him. "You always say we are to blame. You always say you are going to leave us and be happy. So now go. Leave us as you say, and let us have some peace." He stared at me for a long time. Then he picked up his things and walked out the door.

I was the one who put Father out, but I was also the one who went to take care of him a few months later when he fell seriously ill. I cleaned his apartment, cooked for him, and did everything possible to ease his suffering as he grew steadily worse. He died in my arms. Oh, what a terrible thing—the expression on Father's face when he died! I shudder to recall it even now. Frustration, hatred, and despair were written there. His last words were curses. With my whole being I resolved I would search for the answer to life's puzzle and find peace so I would not have to die a death like Father's.

Elena

Life must have been hard for Mother when we were little. In those days the four of us lived in a tiny room. The bathroom was down the hall, as was the kitchen, which she had to share with another woman who would constantly dirty our things and throw out our food. But if life was hard or she felt frustrated, she never let us know. She loved to sew, and she always kept us scrubbed and spotless. She dressed us well and taught us to love beauty.

On washdays Mother would scrub our clothes in a little galvanized tub and wring them out. Then she would carry them out the door and down the hall to a little metal staircase that went up and up to an attic room where she would hang them up to dry. Of course, this room, with its hazardous stairway, was off-limits to little girls.

I was only about 3 or 4 and did not understand what Father was telling us about searching for the meaning of life, but it seemed to me that whatever it was, it must be up there in that little room where Mother would go with our clothes.

One day Mother forgot to lock the door after she came back to our room to wash still another tubful of clothes. In a flash I slipped out and ran for those stairs. An instant later I stood trembling and breathless at the doorway that I thought would lead me to find the meaning of life. Oh, what a disappointment! I can remember it so well. There was just this dark room. The floor was littered, and there was dust everywhere. I looked around, shattered. Then I saw it—a shaft of brightness poured into the room at one end. My eyes followed the shaft up to its source. It was a skylight, a small window in the roof high overhead that provided the only light for that dismal room. *So that is where it is*, I thought. *Up there is the meaning of life.* But it was still far above, as unreachable as ever.

I was still gazing at the skylight, transfixed, when Mother came rushing into the room and grabbed me. She had been frantically looking for me. She still says it is a miracle I did not fall to my death from those dangerous stairs.

Both Ala and I caught something of Mother's love of beauty. We also loved to sew, and when we finished the equivalent of junior high school, we enrolled in technical school to study sewing and clothing design.

After finishing technical school with honors, I enrolled in the university to study design. I felt that this would be the place where I could develop my talents. And things did go well. I continued to earn top grades and won a number of prizes. I even had opportunities to appear on television and represent the university at fashion and design congresses in different parts of the country.

But still I found life to be filled with far more disappointments than joys. Everything seemed to be so meaningless. In order to design for people, it is necessary to study them closely. This study proved especially interesting, and it seemed to me that everywhere I looked, I found people as empty and frustrated as I was. I was no longer looking for the meaning of life in the attic, but it still seemed as elusive and as far away as when I was a little girl.

Ala

We were at a party when I first saw Mario. From across the room I noticed his wavy black hair and aristocratic features. A bevy of girls flocked around him, and when he flashed one of his frequent smiles, it was as though someone had turned on the sunshine. One of the girls whispered to me that he was from Cuba and was studying international journalism at the University of L'viv. Before long he made his way to where I was sitting and introduced himself. We spent the rest of the evening together. When the party was over, Mario wanted to escort me home, and as we left together I noticed how careful he was to help me into my coat, hold the door for me, and help me into the taxi. I had never been treated so courteously in my life.

When we arrived home, Mario asked to meet my mother. Soon he was sitting in our tiny living room and Mother was smiling and blushing while Mario admired her handicraft and beautiful wall decorations and enjoyed the Russian sweets she offered him.

It was not only I who fell in love with Mario; the whole family loved him even before I did—Mother, Elena, and all my cousins, aunts, and uncles. He charmed them all. After that no family gathering was complete without Mario—he was always the life of the party.

Soon Mario spoke of taking me back to Cuba with him, and in my dreams I envisioned a green paradise in the Caribbean where the birds sang all day long and cold, gray winters never came. It did not take me long to decide, but even before I gave my answer, my family enthusiastically urged me to accept.

Marriage across the lines of such vastly different cultures as Cuban and Ukrainian is a hazardous undertaking at best. Unfortunately, neither Mario nor I had the spiritual foundations that might have made it work. After a few months in the marriage I was convinced that I had made a serious mistake.

Mario had mentioned that we would be staying with his parents until we could get an apartment. I did not realize that in Cuba this usually means years of waiting. Mario's parents no doubt had good intentions. They wanted the best for their son. They had had serious doubts about his marrying a foreign girl, and when he brought me home and they discovered my ways were so different from theirs, and I could speak only a few words of their language, their fears seemed to be fully justified. As my frustration and sense of desperation grew, so did their hostility.

Mario and I did finally get an apartment, but by that time too many other things were wrong, and there was no way to save the marriage. Shortly after our little girl was born, we got a divorce.

Some of the darkest days of my life followed our separation. I began to fear I was losing my mind. I had a job working at a clothing factory and was making good wages, but I had to leave my little girl each morning in a daycare center and go to work.

Finally, I was able to save enough for a trip back to the Ukraine to visit my family. I hoped that this would bring relief from the pain and sorrow, but nothing seemed to help. Mother had loved Mario so much that she seemed to blame me for what had happened. Every day I would cry and wonder what life held in store.

I had contracted asthma while in Cuba, and after I'd returned home this had turned into a harsh cough that often left me gasping for breath. As a result, my chest was sore, and breathing was painful.

One day the skies were dark, and it was pouring rain. My spirits were especially low. In spite of this I suddenly got the notion of going to visit some friends on the opposite side of the city. Mother was alarmed. "Why don't you wait for better weather," she urged.

"No," I said, "I'm going." And off I went.

As the trolley bus splashed its way through the rain-swept streets, I sat with my face glued to the window. In the seat just ahead of me was a woman who was also looking out at the torrents of rain. "What a rainy day," she said softly.

Maybe it was the gentleness of her voice that attracted me to this woman. Or maybe it was her clean, wholesome appearance and quiet demeanor; I don't know. Anyway, we began talking. This was unusual for me, because Mother always taught us not to speak with strangers. But in a few minutes I found myself pouring out my heart to this kind woman, who listened sympathetically.

"You must come home with me," she said. "My sister is an expert at therapeutic massage and other simple treatments, and I am sure she can help you feel better." Mother would have thought I had taken leave of my senses, but without a moment's hesitation I dropped the plans to visit my friends and agreed to go home with this woman. On the way she told me that she did not actually live in L'viv. She was from Chernobyl and was one of the thousands of people who were forced to leave that city because of the nuclear accident there. She was staying temporarily with her sister in L'viv.

Her sister was indeed an expert at massage. She also applied hot fomentations to my chest and back, and in a short while I was breathing more freely and feeling better than I had for a long time. But the most marvelous change was in my spirit. Those dear women poured out love on me, and my sad and broken heart just soaked it up.

As I was leaving, I tried to pay for the treatments, but they smilingly told me to put away my purse. "You must come back tomorrow for another treatment," they said. "We want to get that condition completely cleared up." I was amazed beyond words. I had never met such people my entire life. When I left their home, it seemed I was stepping into a different world. The rain still drizzled from the low overcast clouds, but to the east a clear patch of blue was showing, and for me the sunshine had definitely returned.

The time was nearly at hand for my return to Cuba, but I was eager that Mother should meet these kind people before I left, so a few days later Mother, Elena, and I called on them. Mother was as pleased with them as I had been. There seemed to be an instant affinity of spirits between them. I had expected this would be the case; they were like Mother in a lot of ways.

But Mother was more perceptive than I had been. Before leaving, she asked, "Are you, by any chance, religious people?"

They nodded and smiled broadly. "Yes," they said, "we are religious."

Elena

After Ala returned to Cuba, Mother and I continued to enjoy the friendship of these wonderful women. We admired their unfailing kindness. They seemed to be at peace with themselves and the world. It was not that they led charmed lives; like everyone else, they had their share of sorrow and problems. But there was something about them that was different. Mother and I talked it over and decided that it was their genuineness that impressed us most. They were real inside and out, and that was a refreshing contrast with so much of what we were used to in social relationships.

One day our new friends invited us to share a meal in their home. What a wonderful time we had. We laughed and told stories about our families. After the meal we stood around the piano and sang. There was a lovely girl who was about my age. She sang a song that was different from any I had ever heard before. It was about God's great love. I didn't know such music existed. It seemed to go through my whole body, and when the music finished, my eyes were wet with tears.

After a while our friends said, "There is a special program this afternoon at our church that we think you would enjoy. Won't you go with us?" We were glad to accept.

When we arrived at the place of worship, I noticed a sign saying "Seventh-day Adventist Church." This meant nothing to me, for I had never heard of any such religion. But when we entered the door, I sensed something I had never felt before. I felt that at last my heart had come home.

After that it required little urging on the part of our friends to persuade Mother and me to go with them regularly. We were amazed as the pastor opened the Bible in his sermons. I had heard of the Bible, of course. In school they told us that it was a collection of fables that had been used in the past to terrify the ignorant masses and keep them in subjection. Now I was discovering a whole new book.

Mother knew more about the Bible than I did. In fact, her father had been a Baptist lay preacher who held religious meetings in his home during the Stalin era, when it was very dangerous to do so. But somehow she had gotten the idea that religion was a list of rules and restrictions that cut you off from the best things in life. Now, as the pastor opened the Book in his sermons, every week was a new revelation of light. We learned about a God whose love is painted in bold letters, who is not content with sitting on some far-off heavenly cloud, but who really cares about us and involves Himself in our lives every day.

One day the pastor gave us a book to read called *The Foundations of Christianity*. It told the experience of a young Communist who had come to have faith. This book helped me understand more about God and about the struggle between good and evil. I was impressed with the beauty and the logic of the Bible's answers to life's great questions. I came to understand that God is the true source of all life and that apart from Him there is no life at all.

At the end of the book it said, "And now it is for you to decide. What will you do with this God who loves you so much? Will you choose God and life and peace, or will you choose eternal death? Those are the true alternatives."

And I said, "Yes, Lord, I choose You."

Soon Mother, too, was reading the book, and I waited eagerly to see what she would say. Finally she put it down and sat quietly for a while. There was a faraway expression on her face. Then she said, "Yes, what it says is true. I am going to choose God." I had never known such happiness as I felt that night.

This decision did not mean all our problems were over. But now we were united in Christ, and we had the assurance that our sins were forgiven. The days seemed to speed by after that. Every afternoon, as soon as the dishes were washed and things were cleaned up, Mother and I would sit down at the table, open our Bibles, and study.

We had been attending the Adventist church for a few months when one Saturday we were electrified by the news that some visitors from Cuba would be presenting the message at the worship service the following week. They were Pastors Juan Guerrero, Julián Rumayor, and Onelio Ara, officers of the union of Seventh-day Adventist churches in Cuba. They were on an official visit to the Soviet Union and were stopping at L'viv as the final point on their itinerary before returning to Cuba.

As soon as the sermon was over, Mother asked for an interview with the visitors, and through a translator, she told them that she had a daughter living in Havana. The pastors took down Ala's address and promised to visit her as soon as they got back to Cuba.

Ala

Mother's letters had given no hint that she was attending religious meetings. She was afraid to put such information in a letter. She only wrote that she and Elena were enjoying the friendship of the wonderful people I had introduced them to and that she would tell me more about it when we could talk.

Elena, too, was guarded in her letters, but she wrote that the most important thing in life was to seek God, to serve Him, and love Him. She sent me a religious poem by a famous Russian poet whose works were formerly banned. I liked what she wrote, although it seemed a bit strange. Then I laid her letters aside and soon forgot all about what she had said.

All this time I felt so empty; everything seemed meaningless. I was questing, hungering, and thirsting for something, but I didn't really know exactly what it was or how to go about finding it.

Although we were divorced, I still saw Mario frequently. One day I asked him if he could get me a Bible. A few days later he brought me a nicely bound Spanish Bible. By this time I had a limited vocabulary of conversational Spanish, but the words in the Bible were so different that I found them almost impossible to understand. For a while I struggled to read with the help of a Spanish–Russian dictionary, but it was discouraging. I could see no sense or profit in what little I did understand. Finally it occurred to me that it might be sacrilegious to use a dictionary to read such a sacred book. So I put the Bible aside and abandoned all attempts to read it.

But still the restless searching continued. I was very unhappy, reaching out for something that always remained beyond my grasp. *Why are we here? What sense does it make?* Again and again I asked Mario what he thought about my questions until he assured me that I had lost my mind. Often I would go outside at night and pray, but not to God. I still didn't have any such concept clear in my mind. I would pray to the air, to the stars, to the grass. I told them I wanted to understand the meaning of life and find peace.

Then, one day, there was a knock on my door. When I opened it, three smiling strangers greeted me. They introduced themselves, and to my amazement, they said they had recently talked with my mother in L'viv. They handed me a letter from her and a gift she had sent of perfume and some socks for my little girl. After a short friendly visit, they left, but not before writing down their address and urging me to visit their seminary.

I placed the paper on a table in front of an open window. A moment later there was a gust of wind, and the paper fluttered off the table to the floor. I pulled back a chair and bent over to pick it up, but the paper was nowhere in sight. Mystified, I pulled out the other chairs and moved the table. Soon I had moved practically everything in the room. I got a broom and swept thoroughly. My search eventually extended to the entire apartment, but the little paper never did reappear.

The visitors had said they were from the Seventh-day Adventist Church. In Mother's letter that the visitors brought, she mentioned this same strange-sounding church name and said that in the Adventist Church she had found greater peace and happiness than she had known in her entire life. The name "Adventist" meant nothing to me, but I assumed it must be a particular order or branch of the Roman Catholic Church. At any rate, I was deeply impressed with these clean, wholesome visitors who looked me straight in the eye as we spoke, and I was determined to follow up on their invitation.

The visitors had told me they were located in a Havana suburb called Boyeros. When Mario first brought me to Cuba, we lived for a time in Boyeros, and I was well acquainted with the area. I thought it shouldn't be hard to find them, and one fine day I set out on my mission to locate their church. Arriving in Boyeros, I soon located the picturesque old Catholic chapel on a quiet side street. There was no sign of a name written anywhere on the building, but I thought, *This has to be the place,* so I knocked on the huge wooden doors.

After a while a woman called from across the street and asked what I wanted. I told her I was looking for the priest, and she said, "The priest who looks after this church doesn't live here. He lives in Santiago and comes only once in a while for Mass."

Disappointed, I returned to my apartment and gave up all hope of any further contact with the kind people whose visit had impressed me so much.

Not long after this a letter from Mother brought exciting news—she was coming to visit. She arrived on September 5, 1987. After the excitement of greeting was over and we were settled in my apartment, Mother brought out a small package and handed it to me. It was a Russian Bible. I clasped it to my heart and said, "This is the best present I have ever received in my life."

About a week after that, to our great joy, the Adventist pastors returned and left us the address of their church. The following Sabbath found us overwhelmed with the warmth and friendliness of the church congregation. It seemed as if everyone wanted to embrace and welcome us. Soon they were announcing from the platform that there were visitors from the Soviet Union. Pastor Rumayor explained how they had first met Mother in L'viv. Then they invited us to the platform, shook our hands, and welcomed us once again.

Back at home Mother brought forth a stack of thick notebooks from her luggage. Since first beginning to attend the church in L'viv, she had taken copious notes on every sermon, every Sabbath school lesson, and every afternoon Bible study session with Elena. She had this information carefully organized in her notebooks. I was supplementing my income by sewing, so every evening after work and supper, I would get out my sewing, and Mother would get out her notebooks and study with me. That became the pattern of our evenings. I would sew while Mother read aloud from her notebooks, giving her own comments and explanations of the lessons. Often she would look up texts in the Russian Bible and read them to me.

We continued to go to church, and I must have heard some excellent sermons during that time, but I will admit that I remember very little from them. What did impress me and what I will never forget were those wonderful evenings at home with Mother. Night after night, as with the disciples of old, my heart would burn within me as she opened the Scriptures and explained their meaning. The long, sad evenings I had previously spent alone were a thing of the past, and the hours seemed like minutes. Often it would be very late when we would finally shut off the lights. And even then I would sometimes lie in the dark and think about the things I was learning from the Bible.

On the Sabbath of December 30, 1989, Mother and I were baptized and became members of the Guanabacoa Seventh-day Adventist Church in Havana.

Elena

I was glad that Mother decided to visit Ala and share with her the beautiful truths we were learning from the Bible, but her leaving was the beginning of a time of struggle and darkness for me. I was depressed, and although I continued attending the Adventist church, I felt as lonely *at* church as I did *away* from it.

Maybe the problem existed only inside of me, I don't know, but the fact is that I felt everyone at the church had friends except me. The youth group fellowshipped together, but I was a little older than most of them and had been married, so I could not identify with them. There was a nice group of young married people, but I was no longer married, so I did not feel comfortable with them either. I continued to attend services, but I was discouraged and felt strongly tempted to give up altogether.

One night I prayed, "Lord, please send me a friend. I need a friend so much, someone I can talk with and who will understand how I feel and help me. Please, Lord, send me someone."

And He did. The next week at church the pastor approached me and said a young woman had come from Moscow to have surgery in L'viv and needed a place to stay. Would there be any possibility she could stay with me? There would indeed!

Sveta turned out to be a true Christian. Like me, she was a convert to the faith, but she had been in the church for five years and understood much more than I did. We prayed and shared and studied together, and we talked for hours about our hopes and plans for the future.

While Sveta studied the Bible with me, I studied Sveta. She probably had no idea how closely I was watching her, but from Sveta I discovered that Christianity is much more than just a happy feeling. It is more than having the right information about God, and certainly, it is more than a set of rules for good behavior. A Christian is a person who has a love relationship with Jesus Christ. Sveta had that kind of relationship. She was in love with Jesus, and this love was reflected in everything about her. She was truly a "loving and lovable Christian." She stayed with me for 10 days, and what a blessing she was to me! God sent her just when I desperately needed a friend. I praise His holy name.

During this time I was invited to the wedding of a family member. While at the reception, I enjoyed visiting with my cousin Igor. Afterward he accompanied me home to carry a watermelon for Sveta. Soon the three of us were sitting around the kitchen table, and Sveta began to tell Igor about Christ.

He had many questions. He was convinced of the bankruptcy of materialism but had no idea where to turn for answers. Now he was hearing answers that came with assurance and clear reasoning. Often Sveta would read from the Bible, and Igor would lean forward eagerly, trying to see the words she was quoting. He was amazed that such an "outmoded" book could contain answers that responded to his deepest questionings. What a blessed evening that was!

The next Sabbath Igor attended church with us. The members were thrilled to see this tall, good-looking young man at church. They welcomed him with rejoicing, and after that I felt more welcome as well.

After his conversion Igor was more than just a cousin; he was a true brother in Christ. We met every day to share and study the Bible. We began to visit our family and friends and talk to them about the gospel.

One Sabbath a few weeks later the pastor, at the close of his sermon, asked anyone who wanted to join God's remnant and prepare to meet Jesus to stand. I bowed my head and prayed. It was a hard struggle. I enjoyed learning about the Bible, but was I really ready to leave everything behind—everything—and follow Jesus? Then I thought of the changes that had occurred in my life over the past few months, of the joy and the peace, the new sense of purpose, the fellowship . . . so many things. And suddenly it became clear to me that apart from Jesus Christ life has no meaning at all. With tears in my eyes, I stood, praying silently.

Suddenly a fear entered my mind. *I wonder what Igor thinks of all this.* Since he had only recently begun to attend, I was afraid he would be upset or turned off by it. I dabbed at my eyes with a handkerchief and hoped he wouldn't be too embarrassed by what I was doing. As discreetly as possible, I turned to look a few pews behind me to where he was sitting. Maybe I could read his reaction from his face. *Oh, joy! Lord, is it really possible? Igor is standing too!* His eyes were shining. Igor and I were baptized a few weeks later on what qualifies as the happiest day of my life.

Igor and I soon discovered that no one is born "grown up." Christian growth is a slow and sometimes painful process. I longed to have perfect peace and perfect trust and love for God and others, but I found many times that my old nature was still alive. At times I would be despondent and easily annoyed.

Igor and I talked over our spiritual problems and decided to put ourselves in the Lord's hands with a 21-day fast. We committed to eating a limited amount of simple foods each day and dedicating hours to prayer, study of the Word, and sharing with others.

Igor had a special reason for prayer. Before becoming a Christian, he had fathered a child. He was definitely not attracted to the child's mother, but now as a Christian he began to wonder what responsibility he had toward his little girl. We decided to pray that he would receive clear guidance from the Lord on this matter.

As we fasted and prayed, Igor became convicted that as a Christian he had a responsibility toward his child that could not be fulfilled simply by offering financial help. He began to visit his little girl and show her fatherly love. Her sweet, innocent heart responded and opened to him as a flower to the sun.

And to Igor's immense surprise, the "impossible" happened. As the weeks went by, he discovered that he was learning to love her mother as well, and she was responding. But the best part was that she was also falling in love with this Jesus whom Igor kept telling her about so enthusiastically. Now they are married and united in Jesus' love.

All this was taking place during a time of great changes in our country. The breakup of the Soviet Union brought a new situation not only to the Ukraine but also to the church. It was a time of revival. Many young people came to know Christ and began actively sharing their faith. For the first time it was possible to put on concerts in the streets with loudspeakers, and people flocked to listen. There were Groups of Mercy that visited the children's hospital to sing and tell stories. How those children loved to listen! They loved to hear about Jesus. Other groups visited the prisons, and a number of notorious criminals found peace and a new life in Christ.

Mother and I were among the many volunteers who came from all over the Soviet Union to help renovate the seminary building at Zaoksky. Oh, to see the joy and enthusiasm of that group. Mother and I made draperies for the chapel and robes for the international choir. What fellowship we enjoyed during those days! We worked hard, and yet it seemed nobody wanted to stop.

We have shared our story as a testimony to the goodness of God and the peace He has brought into our lives. Indeed, "the good hand of our God [has been] upon us" (Ezra 8:18).

Of one thing we are very sure: there is no happiness such as the happiness that comes from knowing Jesus. This is the only reality that matters. And this is what Father so often told us to look for. And last, we have found it—we have discovered the true meaning of life.

Chapter 9

The Change From 10 Centavos

. . . .

Grace Hackett Lake

Willis Hackett, president of the Adventist Church in the northern Philippines, and his wife, Margaret, were enjoying a few days of vacation in the picturesque city of Baguio. Contented and relaxed, they strolled through the public market admiring the beautiful handicrafts that are typical of the region.

Just then Willis looked up to see a child who was heading straight toward them. "See that girl?" Willis asked his wife. "She's a beggar, and she's going to ask us for money."

"How do you know?" asked Margaret.

"You can always tell, because they wear clothes that are at least two sizes too big for them. And they think all Americans are rich. We'll just ignore her and see what she does."

"Agreed," said Margaret.

They kept walking, paying no attention to the outstretched hand, but the little girl did not give up easily. She took hold of Willis's coattail and pulled it.

He turned and asked, "What do you want?"

"Please, sir, could I have five centavos? I haven't had any breakfast."

Reaching into his pocket, Willis brought out a handful of change and gave her the smallest coin he had, a 10-centavo piece.

The little girl scurried away and soon disappeared in the crowd. The missionary couple continued their walk, enjoying the colorful displays in shops along the way. Twenty minutes later they had almost forgotten about the incident, when they saw the same little girl heading straight for them once again.

"You were an easy mark, Willis," said Margaret. "Now she's coming back for more."

"Right. We'll just ignore her again and see what she does this time." Looking straight ahead, they again brushed past the outstretched hand, and once again the child used the same tactic to get their attention.

They turned to face her. "What do you want this time?"

"Mister, here's your change. I asked you for five centavos, remember? And you gave me 10."

Astonished, Willis and Margaret asked her, "Where do you live, child? Who are you? What does your father do?"

After answering their questions, the girl said, "Come with me."

They followed little Feley (not her real name) to a hut on poles among many other such hovels. They climbed the narrow ladder to the thatched rooms. When their eyes adjusted to the dim light, they were appalled at what they saw. In one corner of the room the father lay on a pile of rags. He was wracked by violent coughing spells, and each spasm brought up bloody sputum. Because his tuberculosis had reached such an advanced stage, he was no longer able to work or care for his family.

The dejected, careworn mother rocked hopelessly back and forth as she attempted to nurse a sickly infant. Eight other children stared at their American visitors, their sunken eyes and swollen stomachs a silent testimony to their constant enemy—hunger.

"How much food do you have in the house?" Margaret asked.

"About a cupful of rice," the mother responded. "That's all."

Immediately these ambassadors for Jesus said, "We'll be right back." They climbed down the ladder and returned to the marketplace where they had met Feley. There they filled two large bags with food: rice, beans, powdered milk, fruits, and vegetables—as much as both of them could carry. Then they hastened back to the dismal room on stilts. After struggling up the ladder with their heavy sacks, they set the food before the astonished family. The children, ecstatic to see so much food, danced around, all talking at once.

Before leaving, Pastor Hackett prayed, "Dear Lord, if it be Thy will, lay Thy healing hand on the husband and father in this family and restore his health and usefulness. Bless this dear burdened mother and these precious children. May we all meet in Thy kingdom. Amen."

Next the Hacketts contacted the Adventist Dorcas Society of Baguio and gave them the address of Feley's family, telling them about their great need, and the Philippine Dorcas women went to work.

After a few more days in the cool mountain air of Baguio, the missionary couple returned to metropolitan Manila to continue their work.

When Willis and Margaret completed their term of missionary service, they returned to the United States to educate their children, but about 10 years later Willis (by then a vice president of the world church) returned to Manila. The teachers at Philippine Union College remembered him fondly and invited him to speak for their chapel service. In his message Willis told about his encounter with Feley.

While he spoke, he noticed a stirring in the back of the auditorium. When Willis was about to sit down, the platform chair brought a young woman to the podium and said, "Pastor, here's the epilogue to your story. This is Feley. She is now a nursing student at our college, and all the members of her family have united with the Seventh-day Adventist Church.

After the service, Willis asked Feley hesitantly, "How is your father?"

"My father has recovered," she answered. "He is working and is a church member also."

"It's a modern-day miracle," Willis responded.

"The food you brought and your prayer gave us hope. Your visit changed our lives."

"Praise God for that," said the pastor, "but the miracle began when you brought us the change from 10 centavos."

Chapter 10

Aren't You Afraid?

. . . .

Jevana Ben Maseko

Lately I have been looking back to those difficult years when we were fighting to free Zimbabwe from its colonial masters. My friends and I were moved by powerful convictions that burned like fire in our hearts. From childhood I learned to hate oppression and tyranny. When I discovered the principles of equality and social justice taught by Communism, it seemed to me that this philosophy offered the best hope of bringing about an equitable society.

At the same time, I viewed religion as a tool colonial powers had used for exploitation. Therefore, I wanted no part of it. After Zimbabwe achieved independence, I served in the army for several years, then retired to serve the government as a civilian. When I served as deputy minister, provincial governor, and later as my country's ambassador to Algeria and Russia, we often had to deal with complex and difficult problems.

Although I still disliked capitalism, socialism seemed to be crumbling before our eyes. I had a sense of disappointment as the idealism of my youth faded away. On a personal level it became increasingly clear that something was missing in my life. I was beset by personal problems, and gradually the conviction came that some of these problems might be solved in some way by religion. I also thought of my achievements and became convinced they were not of my own doing.

In 1994, when I was serving in Algeria, my personal problems came to a head. One day I felt an exceedingly strange sensation, as if something was urging me to pray. That evening I knelt alone next to my bed and prayed aloud. The act gave me a sense of peace. When my family returned I prayed silently so they would not know about my communication with God. I know God answers prayer because from that day on the solutions to my problem became clearer and clearer.

In 1995 I was transferred to Moscow, and there I had an administrative assistant, Eddie Goniwa, who had earned a reputation for efficiency and integrity. I was not warned ahead of time that Goniwa was a Seventh-day Adventist. This fact soon became apparent, however, because Eddie was a persistent witness. Apparently, this was not something he specifically tried to do; instead, it seemed to just be part of who he was. In ways that seemed perfectly natural, Eddie's faith often came up in our conversations. Every morning Eddie would come into my office bringing documents that needed my attention. I liked his cheerful ways and enjoyed chatting with him before getting on with the activities of the day.

As we got better acquainted, I sometimes joked with Eddie about his faith. Because he was so likeable, I never found his witnessing offensive. But at the same time, I wanted him to know there was no possibility he was going to influence me to think the way he did. "Furthermore," I told him, "I like my pork, cigarettes, and alcohol too much. Even if I decided to join a religion, it would have to be one that lets me have a little freedom."

Eddie never argued. He just smiled. Then after a while he'd come at me again from a different angle. They say that water can wear away the hardest rock. Maybe something like that happened to me. As time went on, my attitude began to soften. I'm not sure at what point I began listening to Eddie, but finally his witness began to influence my thinking.

Eddie sensed this change, and sometimes when serious problems came up, he would say, "General Maseko, why don't we pray about this?" Then we would stop what we were doing and he would pray.

This was the way things were in 1998 when I became seriously ill. "You have amyloidosis," the doctors told me. "Your bone marrow is producing a type of protein that your body is unable to metabolize. As a result, there is an excess of it in your system." They told me the disease is incurable and usually fatal, but they recommended that I see specialists at Boston Medical Center in the United States to receive the best possible analysis of my condition and latest treatment.

Eddie and his wife visited me at home and prayed with me. Just a few years earlier this would have been unwelcome, but at that point it was a deeply meaningful act. They also accompanied me to the airport. "We will continue praying for you," they told me, "and so will the whole church." I was powerfully moved.

As the doctors in Boston continued to conduct tests and study my case, their faces were always grave. Before long my principal physician came into my room with another man whom I had never met.

My doctor said, "General Maseko, you need to know that you are seriously ill. There is very little chance that you will recover. We're going to start you on chemotherapy, which in itself is dangerous and may take your life."

"I understand," I said. "I am prepared."

The doctor looked doubtful. "This man is a psychologist; he wants to talk with you."

The psychologist started in. He had a little notebook, and he wrote down my answers as we talked. After a while, he stopped and said, "You're a desperately sick man. It's likely you will die; yet you seem strong. Aren't you afraid at all?"

"No," I said, "I'm not afraid."

"Why not?" he wanted to know.

"Because God is with me; my life is in His hands. Whatever He does, whatever He decides, is satisfactory with me. If He sees that I can be of service, that I can still be useful, then I will live."

The psychologist looked into my face for a long moment. Then he closed his notebook and walked out.

I think my faith saved my life. I had a sense of freedom and peace; and instead of dying I slowly began to improve. When the doctors in Boston were ready to release me, they sat me down for a serious talk. "First of all, you have to stop using alcohol and tobacco," they said. "You must strictly limit your intake of fat and flesh foods, and you have to eat lots of fruits and vegetables. You must also walk several miles every day."

I smiled, because I was thinking, *They're telling me I have to join Eddie's church. I'm going to become a Seventh-day Adventist.*

But when I got back to Moscow, I didn't tell Eddie about my decision; I thought he would take credit for having converted me. So I kept my convictions to myself. But soon I had an occasion to return to Zimbabwe. Instead of staying with friends whom I usually visited in Harare, I went to the home of my nephew, who is a Seventh-day Adventist minister. He and his wife could hardly believe it, but they made me feel welcome.

One day I told my nephew I wanted to go to church with him on Saturday to listen to his sermon. This gave him a moment of consternation because in our culture my nephew simply could not be the one taking his uncle to church. So he discussed the matter with the late R. R. Ndlovu, one of the long-serving ministers and great leaders of the church in the former Eastern Africa Division. This dear man of God came to the house on Saturday and escorted me to church. When we entered the building, the people were singing. I immediately felt at home and enjoyed it from beginning to end.

Upon returning to Moscow, I told Eddie about my decision and began to attend the Adventist church with him on a regular basis.

Not long after this the government asked me to become ambassador to Cuba. "Are there Seventh-day Adventists in Cuba?" I asked Eddie. He didn't know, but he went off, and soon he was back with a big smile.

"I looked on the Internet," he said, "and here's what I found." He had checked the Web page of the Inter-American Division and brought me a list of addresses of the principal churches and the administrative offices of the Adventist organization in Havana.

My first Saturday in Cuba found me at the Marianao Seventh-day Adventist Church, which became the church I attended the entire time I was in Cuba. There was such a joyful spirit in the congregation. I loved the enthusiastic singing, as well as the friendly smiles, handshakes, and hugs.

Soon the pastor began coming to my house to study the Bible with me. I joined the church by baptism in February 2001. Even after that, I asked the pastor to continue to come and study with me because I wanted to be strongly grounded in the teachings of Scripture. Now I understand Eddie Goniwa better. When you find something good, you naturally want other people to know about it. Often at church they announce plans for a group to go out in the afternoon to visit the sick or elderly and bring them a word of encouragement. I love to go along, not as the ambassador from Zimbabwe, but as an ambassador of God's kingdom, eager to share His great love with others.

A video was made of my baptism, and I sent copies of it to my brothers and other family members and friends in Zimbabwe, because I want them, too, and everyone else, to know how good the Lord has been to me and what a blessing it is to be a member of God's family on earth and a candidate for living with Him one day in heaven.

Chapter 11

Do You Think There Is No Way Out?

. . . .

Carmen Hernández[1]

The bus moved rapidly through the streets of the little city, and within a few minutes it was on the long dusty road that ended at the beach. It was a beautiful scene; the blue of the sea melted into the blue of the sky, and in the distance the sun was sinking toward the horizon as the clouds took on fiery hues of orange and red.

But the young mother, absorbed in dark thoughts, was not thinking about the natural beauty of the place as she looked at her two young daughters: Luisa, who was 2, and 1-year-old Liliana. Burning tears ran down her cheeks, bathing the forehead of little Liliana, who slept peacefully on her lap, feeling secure and never guessing the magnitude of the terrible situation that hovered over their heads.

Suddenly the voice of Luisa drew her out of her thoughts. "Mommy, why are you crying? Does your tummy hurt? I'm hungry, Mommy. When can we eat?"

"Yes, sweetheart, as soon as we get off the bus, I will give you some supper, and you will never, never, be hungry again. I promise."

The bus stopped in the tourist zone, and she got off, carrying Liliana in one arm while holding the hand of Luisa, who walked peacefully by her side.

They walked a long way until they came to an isolated spot where no tourists ever came. There she spread out a white sheet for a tablecloth on the brilliant sand and prepared to serve a large piece of bread to Luisa, but not without first lacing it with a white powder she had brought in her bag. But before she finished, the child, overcome by weariness, was already asleep on the blanket beside her little sister. Carmen took Liliana's bottle and added a generous amount of the same white powder to the milk.

Now she only had to wait for the girls to wake up to give them their last supper, and after that they would go to sleep forever; then she would drink a glass of water into which she had placed an enormous amount of the same poison to make sure she would not remain alive.

She sat there patiently beside her daughters looking at their angelic faces. They were so beautiful! And she loved them so much.

Her eyes rested on the immense sea still tinted with the last light of fading day. The blue-gray clouds seemed to be putting on a special display of majesty and beauty. Unexpectedly her thoughts turned to her childhood and the beginning of a life of suffering and misery.

She could once again hear the angry shouting voices: "I don't want her in my house, Lorenzo! Take her away! Can't you see I already have too many children to take care of? And you're not providing even the most essential things for them!"

"But Josefa," the man answered, "what do you want me to do? Her mother died bringing her into the world, and her father, my friend François, just died of malaria. He made me promise not to abandon his little girl. Let her stay here with us, at least until we can find some place for her. She's so little! She's not even 2 yet."

"All right, but just until you can find a place to send her," answered Josefa. Carmen was too young to understand all that was implied, but somehow she knew they were talking about her.

Then she remembered the words she had heard many times from this woman she always thought was her mother: "You're so ugly, child! No man will ever want you. Hurry up and get that floor mopped and wash the dishes. At least you can do that."

And other times: "Don't eat that food; I made it for my son Rafael! He works hard, unlike you. You just lie around all day. I can't believe it; you're 5 years old, and you're still so useless."

"That scum who brought you here has been gone a long time, as if it were easy for me to feed eight mouths!"

Other times Josefa said: "You stay here and take care of the house. We'll be back maybe tomorrow afternoon. These parties at the Ballesteros' place go on for days, and my daughters need to meet boys their age. Maybe they can get married and get away from this miserable existence. Remember, now, don't go out of the house for any reason. Here are some tortillas and *atole*² that you can eat while you wait for us to come back."

The nights were so long and dark. *Why doesn't my mother love me? Why do my brothers and sisters always exclude me from everything they do? Why do they leave me alone? I am afraid, so afraid!* Little Carmen covered her face with her hands, trying to choke down the terror she felt at being left alone in the isolated country home miles from any other human habitation. She saw monsters in every shadow. The night sounds seemed like the shriek of demons. Even the scurrying insects startled her. The shrill of crickets and locusts, the chatter of monkeys in the forest, the crackling sounds of animals prowling through the woods, the cries from the hen-house when some predator approached, the wild barking of the dogs, and even the flapping wings of the night birds filled her heart with anxiety and fear.

How she longed for a tender kiss from her mother, a caress or at least a kind word! To feel herself enfolded, safe, and protected in her arms. But the only reality in her world was anxiety and a never-ending loneliness. No one seemed to care or even notice her. Many days she felt as if she were invisible. The few dirty rags on the floor on which she slept at night were the only thing that felt like her own. Her only playmates were frogs, crickets, rabbits, and other small creatures of the field, and a few friends who existed only in her imagination.

Very early one morning the shadows of night had not yet disappeared when Carmen felt someone shaking her. "Quick, get up," said one of her older sisters.

"What's happening? What do I have to do?" she asked.

"Nothing! Nothing at all. The nuns have come to take you away. You're going to an orphanage."

"The nuns? Take me to an orpha . . . to a what?"

"To an orphanage, dummy. That's where orphans live. Children like you who don't have a mother or father."

"But I have Mommy and Daddy and you," she stammered, starting to cry. "Who wants to take me away? Where is Mommy? Does she know?"

"Yes, of course she knows. She's the one who sent me to get you. Now hurry. The nuns are waiting."

"Mommy! Oh please, Mommy, don't let them take me away." Carmen was crying hysterically now. "Tell them I'm your little girl; tell them that you love me! I promise not to be naughty anymore or ever do things that make you angry ever again. I'll be good, I promise. Oh, please, Mommy, don't let them take me away." Desperately she clung to her mother's knees, seeking protection. "I love you, Mommy, I love you."

Unexpectedly, there were tears in the eyes of that hard-hearted woman, but the matter was decided, and she was not about to change her mind. Never! The little girl had to go to the orphanage.

"Look, Carmen," she said in a sweeter voice than the child had ever heard before. "You have to go. It's for your own good. In the orphanage you will have plenty of food. You will have a bed of your own and people who will take care of you. Above all, they will prepare you for when you grow up. You are so ugly that you have to learn a lot, because no one will ever want to marry you."

"I don't want to get married, Mommy. I just want to stay here and take care of you, give you kisses, and tell you I love you!"

"Look, Carmen, I am not really your mother. I'm sick all the time and can hardly care for my own children. I know you are intelligent, and although you are little, you will be brave, you will always obey. I'll come to visit you, I promise."

She spoke no more, but turned and hurried into the house and shut the door behind her.

For the first time Carmen realized that Josefa was not her mother, and the news filled her with horror and pain. If this woman was not her mother, who was? Where were her parents? Why had they abandoned her? And these women with strange black clothing and hoods over their heads—who were they? And where were they taking her? So great was her terror that she fainted and fell to the ground. When she revived, she found herself in a bed in a strange room, and a woman who seemed like an angel was putting damp cloths on her forehead.

When the woman saw that Carmen was awake, she smiled and said, "Here, take this, little sweetheart. This nourishing soup is for you. You are so thin and pale. You have had a high fever for many days. We thought you were going to die."

The girl didn't ask any questions. She was too weak and tired. Besides, what was there to ask? Somehow she understood that from this day on this would be her home and her family.

In a few days she was feeling stronger. Then Mother Rosa came for her. She was a very young nun. She said, "Carmen, now that you are well, I am going to take you to your cell and introduce you to your companions and show you your duties." She gave the child a simple uniform and shoes, which she had never worn before, and helped her put them on. Then they went out of the infirmary and walked down the long hallway of the convent, which was surrounded by beautiful gardens with fruit trees, rosebushes, and a great variety of flowers, all of which perfumed the air and made it seem like paradise. They came to a long room where there were eight beds, and Mother Rosa said to Carmen, "That last bed down on the end is yours."

"Mine? A bed of my very own?" asked Carmen in amazement.

"Yes, child. That is where you will sleep from now on. It's not fancy, but it will be comfortable."

To sleep in a real bed seemed like a fairy tale!

"That's . . . wonderful!" stammered the child. "You already showed me where we will bathe, but where is the river or lake where I'll go to bring water for bathing or for washing my clothes with the other girls?"

"No, Carmen, you don't need to carry water for bathing or for anything else. See? It comes right out of a pipe; you just turn this little knob and there it is!"

It was all so new and amazing. Could she be dreaming?

"Now the next thing is for you to meet Mother Superior, who is in charge of this place." She knocked softly on a large door and went in holding Carmen's hand. Mother Teresa looked up from her desk smiling and said, "So this is the new little angel God has sent to live with us. How old are you, child?"

"Eight," said Carmen shyly.

"Eight! I thought you couldn't be more than 6; you are so small and thin. Well, you are welcome, dear child. I hope you are very happy here with us. Now you may go, and Mother Rosa will finish explaining your activities."

Years later Carmen sometimes heard people speak of the orphanages operated by the religious as harsh or even cruel, but her experience was not like that. The nuns were strict but always sweet. She had her own bed. Her clothing was plain but clean, and she was given food three times a day. She went to school in the orphanage. The routine of study, work, and prayers was not a problem for her because her new life was so much better than the previous one.

In fact, it all seemed like a dream, a beautiful dream! In her fantasies the convent seemed like an enchanted castle, and the gardens were beautiful woods, and the bell tower was the pinnacle of the castle. She dreamed that one day a charming prince would come mounted on a white horse and carry her off. They would get married and live happily ever after.

Six years went by. Then one day, when she was 14, the nun who was the doorkeeper came and said to her, "Carmen, your father has come to visit you."

She felt a cold chill run down her back. She had seen the man only a few times when she was little because he was seldom home, and he had never visited her at the orphanage. Why had he come? Would he take her away?

Unwillingly she went out to the visitors' room, and there he was. No longer the fine-looking man she remembered, he was old and disheveled. His few remaining teeth were dark and discolored. The stench of tobacco and sweat was nearly unbearable.

"My dear little daughter!" he said with slurred speech. "You have no idea how much I have missed you. A few days ago I went to visit your mother, and I saw your photo on the shelf, and I said to myself, 'Lorenzo, you've got to go and visit your daughter,' so here you have me."

He talked on and on about things she could not understand, and then he said something that made her shudder with horror. "I have come to take you away because I have given you in marriage to a friend of mine." He is a rich man. He is old, but he has plenty of experience, and I know he will make you happy. Now go call the head of this place, because I need to talk with her."

Trembling and crying, Carmen went to Mother Teresa and gave her the message. She left the visiting area because she was not permitted to be there and hear the older people talk. After about an hour Mother Teresa came to her room. Her face, which had always been sweet, was contorted with anguish and deep anger. "Dear child," she said, "your father will come on Sunday with a man he has chosen to be your husband. You will have a simple dress because there is no time to make anything else. And the wedding will be here in our chapel. Your father wanted to take you today, but I insisted you have to leave here married and with the blessing of God."

"But Mother, I don't . . . Oh Mother, please, please, you've got to protect me. Please don't let them do such a terrible thing to me. Don't let them take me away. Please, have pity; help me!"

"Don't say anything, child. Your father has decided the matter, and we have to accept it. Remember, our religion commands us to obey our parents." She said no more. A knot in her throat made it impossible, and she left hastily as tears started down her cheeks. She had tried in vain to dissuade the man from his evil intentions.

On Sunday the two men arrived promptly, and Carmen, who seemed no more than a small child, appeared dressed in white with a thin little veil on her head and a few white flowers in her trembling hands. These were flowers the girl herself had cared for with much love. Except for the two men, all those present were crying.

Carmen's stepmother and brothers and sisters were not there. They had no knowledge of what Lorenzo had done until a long time later when they went to the convent for their annual visit. Then they had no way to find out where he had taken the girl.

If Carmen believed that she had already known all that was possible of suffering and bitterness in her early years, she was mistaken, because after her wedding day she discovered what it truly was to live a life that is hell on earth. She was a complete slave. She had to obey this man blindly and absolutely. He took great pride in telling her that he had won her in a poker game with her father. Therefore, he was her owner, and she was a piece of furniture, an object that he could break in pieces and throw in the trash anytime he pleased. He kept her locked in a mansion that was truly a fortress. He never allowed her to communicate with her stepmother or the nuns. She had every material thing she might wish for, but her husband was an alcoholic, a drug addict, and a depraved abuser who enjoyed making her suffer the most terrible beatings, insults, and humiliations, things that should never be repeated.

Her daughters, when they were born, were a balm for her tortured soul. She loved them so much. But when their father would come home drunk or high on drugs and begin to physically abuse them, it was even greater torture for her than what he did to her.

One day there was a loud pounding on the iron bars of the gate that opened onto the street. Carmen was never allowed to open the gate or even look to see who had come. The gardener opened it, and when he did, a number of people pushed their way in, shouting and shoving him aside.

With some difficulty she understood them to say that her husband had been killed in an accident. Among the people were three women who all claimed to be his wives, and a number of grown sons and daughters. They grabbed Carmen by her arms and shoved her out onto the street together with her little girls. The cook, realizing what was happening, hastily put three bottles of milk, some diapers, a blanket, two little sheets, and several packages of crackers in a bag. She said: "Here, this will help you for at least a few hours."

Carmen stood in the middle of the street in a state of shock. In all those years she had never been outside the mansion. She had no clear idea of where she was and no knowledge of the streets. At her side were two terrified and crying children, and she was far advanced in her pregnancy with a third. The evictors hadn't allowed her to take any money or personal documents or clothing, even for the little girls.

She first tried to look for protection with some families in nearby houses, but they were afraid and shut their doors. She had no idea of the name of the village where she was born, and even if she had, there was no money for transportation to the place. Walking aimlessly, she came to a church. She thought maybe she could find help or information on how to get in touch with the convent and her beloved nuns. She knocked and called, but the doors were shut. With that, her last hope faded.

Overwhelmed, she fell to the ground sobbing in bitter anguish. When the little girls saw their mother crying, they put their tiny arms around her and cried with her. A few passersby were moved to pity by the sight and tossed her some coins. After Carmen had cried a long time, she noticed the coins. That was when she made the decision to buy rat poison. In her confused and hopeless state of mind, that seemed like the only way out. After purchasing the poison, she got on the bus with her daughters and made her way to the beach.

Carmen was still thinking of all this as she watched her daughters sleeping on the sand.

Just then she heard a clear masculine voice say, " 'Come unto me, all ye that labour and are heavy laden, and I will give you rest.' Are you tired of living? Do you think there is no way out but death? Has life dealt you so many blows that you think you can't stand any more? Do you have not even enough bread left to satisfy your hunger? I have good news for you. You are not alone. The Lord is with you; He is waiting for you with open arms. Come, He is calling you. He will free you from your pain and burdens. He will give you the bread of life, and you will never hunger again. He will give you the water of life, and you will never be thirsty again. He offers you redemption and salvation. He is your Creator; your life belongs to Him."

Carmen's amazement knew no bounds. How could anyone know her life and speak so directly to her situation? She was sure the words were meant for her. Trembling, she stood and walked in the direction from which the voice was coming. She found a group of people seated on the sand listening to a radio program that was just ending. The announcer said that the program was called La Voz de la Esperanza (the Voice of Hope).

A middle-aged couple from the group noticed Carmen standing there. They went to her and, seeing the anguish on her face, spoke to her kindly.

They told her they were Adventist Christians and invited her to join them in the songs, prayers, and other activities of their spiritual retreat.

She told them she needed to go for her children, who were sleeping nearby, and they accompanied her. When she got there, the baby had just awakened and was starting to put the bottle into her mouth. With a leap Carmen reached her and snatched it away. The startled child began to cry. She could not understand why her mother had taken away her milk. "No, child, you cannot drink that. Your life is precious. It belongs to God."

She awakened the older child, took the baby in her arms, and went back to where her new friends received her warmly. They invited her to sit down and join them just as they were handing out fruit and sandwiches. Before eating, they prayed, thanking God for the food and for Carmen and her daughters, who had come to be with them.

The way these people treated Carmen reminded her of the kindness she had received years before from the nuns. She told them about her situation, and the Adventists immediately organized to help her. One of the members invited Carmen and the girls to live with her for as long as she might need it. Others helped her find a child-care center for the girls and a place where she could work part-time. They helped her enroll in a school where she could finish her studies.

Today Carmen is a happy woman, enjoying the blessings of a Christian home. Her children are professionals and married, and all are active members of the Adventist Church.

---

[1] Although she writes in the third person, this is Carmen's own story. Carmen Hernández is a pseudonym, and all names in the story have been changed.

[2] A drink made of corn flour.

Chapter 12

Even a Mule

. . . .

Virgilio Zaldívar

In 1944 I was working as a pastor in Bahía de Mata, near Baracoa, in eastern Cuba. One day I needed to go into Baracoa, and as usual, I rode my mule, Coqueta. There were two paths to the city. One followed along the coast; the other, which went through the mountains, was much more uneven and difficult. I came to the point where the road divided, and naturally, I intended to follow the coastal trail, but Coqueta, for some reason, would not go to the left. I insisted strenuously, but she absolutely refused to obey. Finally, I gave up and let her have her way.

About a half hour later Coqueta abruptly halted and would go no farther. After trying very hard to get her to move, I noticed a house just off the road to the left. I realized then that I was thirsty, so I decided to go up to this house and ask for some water. When I knocked, a woman came to the door with two young girls at her side. She brought the water I requested, but I saw an expression of great sorrow on her face.

"May I know why you are so sad?" I asked.

She told me that her sister had died, and she was inconsolable. The girls, she explained, were her nieces.

"I have a message for you from God," I said.

"Oh, please, come in," she answered. "We need it so much."

I went in and talked to her about Jesus, His second coming, the resurrection, and the glad reunion of the redeemed. Opening my Bible, I shared with her the apostle Paul's beautiful reassurance for those who mourn the loss of a loved one: "For the Lord Himself will descend from heaven with a shout, with the voice of an archangel, and with the trumpet of God. And the dead in Christ will rise first. Then we who are alive and remain shall be caught up together with them in the clouds to meet the Lord in the air. And thus we shall always be with the Lord. Therefore comfort one another with these words" (1 Thess. 4:16-18, NKJV).

I saw a great change in the expression on the woman's face. It was evident she had found peace and hope in the message. She fervently asked me to continue visiting.

From that day on, I visited this woman every two weeks to study the Bible with her. She began attending church with the girls, and when she was ready, Pastor Juan Bautista Salas baptized her.

In 1985 I was in the United States visiting a church in Miami when a woman approached me and explained she was one of those little girls who had been weeping that day over the loss of their mother. It gave me great joy to find her faithful and actively participating in the church after so many years.

This is a living example of how God can work. In reality, He is not limited; even a mule can obey His will and be an instrument of blessing in His hands.

Chapter 13

Beloved Enemy

. . . .

Jiri Drejnar

It was always my desire to serve the Lord in some way, but during the years that the Communists were in power in Czechoslovakia, it was not easy.

During that time I spent two years at a military work camp, and then I worked another two years for the army as a civilian. Four years later, when the church was permitted to conduct limited activities, I served as a pastor. Beginning in 1968, at the time of Alexander Dubček's "Prague Spring," I worked for four years as the editor of the Czech *Signs of the Times* magazine.

In March 1978 the state police (the Czech version of the KGB) called me in and asked me to cooperate with them in providing information about foreign visitors, our believers, church activities, and so forth. When I declined, a number of interrogations followed—each always several hours long. Eventually I was forbidden to work as an editor.

For six months I was unable to find another job because, by order of the state police, no one was allowed to hire me. Finally, in February 1979, I began work in a hospital as a technician.

The head doctor at the clinic—a world-renowned urologist—was not a Communist, and he helped me get a better job. I became the business manager of the clinic one year later, and my wife became the head receptionist.

A few days before Christmas I was informed that a very high state official would be entering the hospital the following day. A day later my wife told me that while she was taking down the necessary information about him, the official made a strange request. He had a large amount of cash on his person, and he asked my wife if she would deposit it in the bank for him. She did as he had requested.

When I visited the man a few days later to see if everything was all right, he told me he would be in the hospital during Christmas and asked if there would be fish for dinner on Christmas Eve (a Czech tradition).

When I told him it would not be possible because there wouldn't be enough for all the patients, he said, "This will be my first Christmas without fish." That evening I told my wife about the situation, and we agreed to prepare fish soup, fried fish, and potato salad for him for his Christmas meal.

On December 24 we went to the clinic and, in the hallway in front of the door to his room, we set out the soup, fish, and even some cookies on a rolling table and wheeled it into his room. He was surprised and deeply touched.

A few days after Christmas I stopped by his room to see him before I left for the day.

The official asked me to sit down on his bed, for he had something to ask me. "Why did you do all of that for me?" he asked.

"You were so sad when you told me that this would be your first Christmas without fish," I answered.

"How long have you been working at this clinic as the director?" he inquired.

"About six months," I offered. "Prior to that I worked as an assistant."

"And what did you do before that?"

"I was the editor of a magazine," I said.

"What kind of magazine?" he inquired further.

"You wouldn't know it," I said. "It was a religious magazine."

"What was the name of the magazine?" he asked again. When I told him the name—*Signs of the Times*—he looked at me with surprise. "What is your name?"

"Drejnar."

"You're Drejnar?" he asked, surprised. "You were a pastor in Plzen, and then you worked in Ostrava. How is it possible that you're here now?"

Now it was my turn to be surprised. Before I answered his question, I asked him, "How is it that you know me, that you even know where I worked?"

"Ever since I was young I have been a confirmed Communist," he began. "When we came to power in 1948, I decided I would fight in the name of the Communist Party against every religion and all churches. I became the head of the department that fought against churches for the state security organization. We decided that we would gradually liquidate all churches and destroy Christianity. The first church we chose was yours—the Seventh-day Adventist Church."

After a brief pause he continued, "It was important to get to know the life of the church members. I bought a copy of the Bible and your hymnal. I lived for a time in the southern part of the country, where no one knew me. I began attending services in various towns. I had been told that visitors in your congregations do not sit down immediately upon entering church; rather, they stand and pray silently for a short while before sitting down. So I was advised to clasp my hands, close my eyes, and count to 25 before sitting down. I visited various families, and we became friends. I got to know many people this way.

"I realized that these were good people and that we would hurt them greatly if we destroyed their church. But it was impossible to do anything else; religion was considered an impediment to progress. It had to be destroyed.

"When we declared all church activities prohibited in 1952, we learned that we had made a big mistake. We were no longer able to keep track of all of you so easily. Where there was once one large church in a town, there were now all of a sudden 10, 15, 20, small groups that secretly met in different homes. We were helpless. That's why we allowed church activities to begin again four years later, and I became the head director of the department that dealt with your church in the secret police administration. I worked there for many years, up to about two years ago, when I was transferred to another position.

"Now I've told you everything about me, so now you tell me why it is that you're here at the clinic and how you got here."

"The state security organization called me in and asked me to cooperate," I began.

"You declined to cooperate," he interrupted, "and that's how you ended up here."

There was nothing more to say or tell him. As I turned to leave, he said: "Mr. Drejnar, I told you I had a Bible that I took with me to church. But I have to admit that I never read it. Could you come sometime with your Bible and read something from it to me?"

"Why 'sometime'?" I asked him. "I can do it today, right now. I have a Bible in my office. I'll get it."

Before I returned with my Bible, I called my wife and explained to her that I was going to be home late because I was about to have a very important conversation with this official. When I returned to his room, I opened my Bible and read John 3:16: " 'For God so loved the world that he gave his one and only Son, that whoever believes in him shall not perish but have eternal life' [NIV]." This was a brief glimpse of God.

Then I read him a passage from the prophecy of Isaiah: " 'We all, like sheep, have gone astray, each of us has turned to our own way; and the Lord has laid on him the iniquity of us all' [Isa. 53:6, NIV]."

When I read these words, I saw tears begin to form in his eyes. But these weren't the only verses I read him that evening. We had a long talk, and at the end I asked him if I could pray with him. He willingly accepted.

We parted with the words: "We will meet again, and soon, I hope."

Because he had cancer and his illness became worse and worse, he remained in the hospital until September. My wife and I visited him almost daily, reading the Bible to him and praying with him. And after a while, he too began to pray. I'll never forget his prayer in which he confessed his animosity toward God, asked for forgiveness, and thanked God for the certainty of salvation.

One Friday afternoon in the middle of September I stopped by to say goodbye for the weekend. "My wife and I are leaving today," I said, "but we'll see you again on Monday morning."

"No, we won't see each other on Monday," he replied. He asked me to call my wife so we could pray together again. Maja came in, I took his hand, and we prayed. I thanked God that I wasn't parting with an enemy of God or His church, but with a brother in Christ and that we could look forward to seeing each other again in a place where there would no longer be pain or death. We parted with the words "We'll meet again—and soon!"

Monday morning the nurse on duty told us that our friend had died on Sabbath morning—not long after our visit.

Today conditions are completely different in the Czech Republic. For almost half a century the Bible was degraded, ridiculed, and almost banned. Today we have religious liberty, we have Bibles, and we can evangelize in public.

This doesn't mean, however, that we don't face any opposition. The outright opposition of a few years ago has been replaced by an indifference to God and His gospel; people are consumed with hatred, greed, and a lack of interest in the needs of others.

Still, the power of God that kept His believers faithful through all the decades of Communism is changing lives and preparing people for eternity. God is trustworthy, and His promises are sure.

"As the rain and the snow come down from heaven, and do not return to it without watering the earth and making it bud and flourish, . . . so is my word that goes out from my mouth: It will not return to me empty, but will accomplish what I desire and achieve the purpose for which I sent it" (Isa. 55:10, 11, NIV).

Chapter 14

Leave Those Silly Fables!

. . . .

Nicolás Chaij

T he first place I was assigned to work as a pastor after graduating from
Plate River College in Argentina was Junín, located in the province of
Buenos Aires.

From the time I arrived in this small city I noticed two young men who
were always together. I didn't know who they were, but I began to pray for
them, hoping that one day I would have a chance to meet them.

One afternoon I heard a knock on my door, and when I opened it,
there they were. "We want to talk with you," they said.

I invited them to come in, but they refused. "No," they said, "we can
talk right here."

And point-blank, with no introduction or preamble of any kind,
they said, "We are active Communists. We support the cause by putting
up posters and giving out handbills. Communism is the solution for the
problems of the world. We're struggling for a just cause, and we have come
to tell you to leave those silly Bible fables and join us."

I had to admire their enthusiasm and sincerity. Once more I invited
them to come in, and again they refused. So I asked them, "Have you ever
read the Bible?"

"No," they answered, "but we have read other books that tell about its
errors, so we know it is not true."

"You are obviously intelligent and well-read," I said to them. "I am sure
you are aware that there was a great empire called Babylon. You also know
that after that came Medo-Persia, followed by Greece and Rome: four
empires that came one after another. And you also know that the fourth
empire, Rome, was divided into the principal nations of Western Europe
today. Isn't that right?"

They nodded. Then I added, "Are you aware that all of that was
prophesied in the Bible 600 years before it happened?"

"All of that is in the Bible?" they asked in amazement.

"Of course. Come in, and I'll show you."

Then they did come in, and I opened the Bible and explained to them the great prophecy of Daniel 2. They were astonished, and because they were sincere young men, they acknowledged the truth of what I said. Enthusiastically they said they wanted to learn more, so we made plans to study the Bible together. A short time later I had the privilege of seeing one of them use his talents as a youth director in our church and the other going door to door sharing the good news of salvation in Christ through the printed page. Thank God, these noble young men had discovered the true cause.

The Prophecy of Daniel 2

Chapter 2 of the book of Daniel foretells the history of the world in the figure of the great image that is made up of four kinds of metal: gold, silver, brass, and iron.

head of gold	Babylon
chest and arms of silver	Medo-Persia
thighs of brass	Greece
legs of iron	Rome
feet of iron and clay	divisions of Europe after Rome, which continue to our day

All this has been fulfilled precisely as foretold. Therefore, we cannot doubt that the near future will bring the fulfillment of the only part of the prophecy that still hasn't happened: that is, a stone that struck the image on its feet and destroyed it. The stone then began to grow until it had filled the whole earth. The explanation of this part is given in the text itself: "In the time of those kings [modern Europe], the God of heaven will set up a kingdom that will never be destroyed, nor will it be left to another people. It will crush all those kingdoms and bring them to an end, but it will itself endure forever" (Dan. 2:44, NIV).

To learn more about this prophecy and others like it, ask for God Cares, *by Mervyn Maxwell (Boise, Idaho: Pacific Press Pub. Assn., 1981, 1985).*

Chapter 15

A Bus to Nowhere

. . . .

Loron Wade

I don't want anybody to get the impression that Juan Cerino is an impulsive man or that he was bored with the work he was doing that day selling Bibles and other Christian books in the Mexican state of Tabasco. But you have to admit that what he did was a bit unusual.

It happened that Juan was going about his usual activities when he had to pass in front of the bus station. Naturally he was hurrying to get away from the noise and contamination that is always present in those places, when suddenly he looked up and saw this gigantic bus sitting there with its engine running, ready to leave. Of course, there is nothing strange or unusual about that, but for some reason Juan turned and, without stopping to think, got on the bus and sat down.

Now, if he had had time to think about it, he probably would have said to himself, "What am I doing here?" and would have gotten back off. But the fact is that he no sooner sat down than the conductor shut the door and away they went.

Where to? Well, Juan didn't have the faintest idea. That was a serious problem, because the conductor was coming down the aisle asking each passenger: "Where to?" And as soon as he heard the answer, he would tear off the corresponding ticket and collect the fare. Seeing this, Juan started to sweat, and not precisely because of the heat. He wished he could shrink in size and become invisible, but this was impossible. Soon the conductor was standing beside him, and it was Juan's turn to answer the question.

"Ah, . . . well, . . . I don't know, that is, I . . ."

The conductor started to scowl. More than once he had had crazies or drunks on his bus, and he knew how to deal with them.

"What did you say? Speak up!" said the conductor, raising his own voice as if to illustrate.

Suddenly Juan's face lit up with an idea, and he dug around in his pocket until he found an undetermined number of coins. He pulled them out and placed them in the conductor's hand, saying, "As far as I can go with this amount of money."

The man shrugged. The expression on his face was eloquent, but he said nothing. He counted out the coins, tore off a ticket, handed it to Juan, and continued with his work.

For some time Juan sat observing the green countryside as the bus wove its way between hills and fields of sugar cane. He had begun to nod off when he felt the conductor tap him on the shoulder. "Here you are," said the man. "You've reached your destination."

Standing beside the highway as the bus took off, Juan looked around, completely bewildered. While he was riding along he had begun to think that maybe the Lord was sending him to another city where he could take a lot of orders. But now he was wondering what had happened, because he was not close to any town. There were not even any houses in sight. The only other human being was a man who was rapidly disappearing in the distance. On one side of the highway there was a cane field and on the other some tall vegetation. In the distance he could hear a dog alternately barking and howling mournfully. Apart from that, there was nothing.

Finally, after a bit more observation, Juan discovered a path that seemed to bore like a tunnel through the dense vegetation, and he started to follow it. Before long he came to a clearing and found a simple country house with stick-and-mud walls and a thatched roof. A man came out of his house shouting to his dogs to calm down before greeting Juan, who was looking around quite surprised. If up to that point all of this had seemed like a strange dream to Juan, he was even more surprised when the man asked, "Are you the one we have been waiting for?"

"I don't know," answered Juan. "Were you expecting someone?"

"Yes, . . . that is, well, not exactly. But I think maybe it's you."

"I don't understand," replied Juan.

"Well, I'm not very sure either. But I have been praying, and now I am expecting someone to bring me what I need."

"What is it you need?"

"Light! That is, an explanation," said the man. "It's just that someone gave us a Bible, and we've been reading it, but there are some things I don't understand. For example, I came across the Ten Commandments, and it says right there plain and simple that we're supposed to rest on the seventh day. I've been looking through the rest of the Bible to see where it says that we no longer need to keep it, or that the day of rest has been changed, but I can't find it."

"And you never will."

"Why not?" said the man. "How do you know?"

"Because there isn't any such text."

"Why? I have been looking and looking, entire days and sometimes far into the night, trying to find where it says we should keep Sunday. And now you come and tell me that there is no such text! What do you know about the Bible?"

"I have read it all many times."

At that, Juan saw the man's eyes fill with tears, and with a broken voice the man said, "Then you really are the one God has sent to us."

"I have no doubt whatever about that," replied Juan. "And now I'm going to ask you something: the Lord has opened your heart and mind to understand this great truth about the Sabbath; what do you plan to do about it?"

"There's no need to ask me what I 'plan' to do. We're already doing it! For four months now my wife and I have not worked on Saturday. But I have had such a desire to talk with somebody; you can't imagine! And now you have come! I just can't believe it!"

The man was shaking his head, deeply moved, when suddenly he reacted and said, "But what are we doing out here? Do come in, please, and if you've brought a Bible, you'd better start pulling it out right now, because I have a lot of things to ask you."

All that day this humble home in the country was illuminated by light from Heaven; and not only that day, because Juan continued to visit and to instruct that fervent seeker for truth. Four months later the man and six members of his family were baptized according to "the commandments of God, and the faith of Jesus" (Rev. 14:12).

Chapter 16

An Unchained Bible

. . . .

Ana Rodríguez de González

My maternal grandfather, Antonio Bazán, was born in Estepona, Andalucía, Spain. As a devout believer, he helped in the work of the church in his town. In the temple there was a large Bible that was fastened to the wall by a chain, because in those days the members of the church were not allowed to read the sacred Book. But when Grandfather was sure no one was looking, he would eagerly read that mysterious volume, and his heart thrilled with its message. How he longed to have a Bible, a Bible of his own, a Bible without chains.

When he was 18 years old, Antonio was called to military service. In those days Cuba was a Spanish colony. The spirit of freedom, which had been stifled during the Ten Years' War (1868-1878), again surfaced. On February 24, 1895, the War of Independence, which would last four years, broke out, and Antonio was sent with the Spanish troops to help put down the rebellion. During the years of struggle my grandfather developed a friendship with many Cubans and tried to help them as much as possible. The island and its inhabitants stole his heart so much that he promised himself he would go back to live in Cuba when the war was over.

When he returned to Spain, he married a young woman named Anna Luna from his town, and he shared with her his dream of returning to Cuba. Soon their first daughter was born, Isabel, who would become my mother; followed by a second, Concepción. Their plans continued to mature, and preparations for the long journey came to their culmination, although there was opposition from both families.

When they arrived in Cuba, my grandparents lived in Cienfuegos. At that time my mother was 3 years old, and her sister 3 months. At first they were poor, but after a few years of sacrifice and hard work they began to prosper.

Seven sons and five daughters were born to them. The oldest was the first to make plans to marry. Her fiancé, Gerardo Rodríguez, came to see her every Sunday, and he saw how the whole family gathered in the living room while my grandmother would read a novel or some other interesting book that friends had lent her.

One day Gerardo brought two books as a present for his future mother-in-law. He said, "A rather strange fellow sold these books to my mother, but at home nobody reads them, so I am bringing them as a gift so you can have something to read in your family gatherings." One of the books was *Practical Guide to Health*, and the other was called *The Coming King*, by Edson White.

Grandmother was delighted to receive the health book, because she was often the doctor in her home and took care of her neighbors as well. How she loved that book! But it was not appropriate to read in the family gatherings, so she decided to begin with the book *The Coming King*. When my grandfather heard what the book said regarding the second coming of Jesus, he said, "That book must be based on Scripture, because that is what the Bible teaches." And he sighed, "If some day we could have a Bible of our own, you would recognize that is what it teaches."

Finally Gerardo and Isabel were married. My sister Micaela was the firstborn, and I arrived two years later. My grandmother's house was situated on a beautiful hill close to the beach. And our house, which was not far from theirs, was at the other side of the crossroads in the highway. Coming from the city, the road on the right led to my grandmother's house, and the one on the left to ours. We often visited our grandparents and enjoyed the company of uncles and aunts.

Time passed without major problems, until the day Grandfather became seriously ill. It was a terrible blow to the whole family when he died. After his death the older sons took over the home, guided by my grandmother, and the entire family continued to gather every evening.

Grandmother was very devout. She had an altar with images of many saints. She was always lighting candles, and many nights she would hold vigils keeping a vow or expressing gratitude for answered prayer. On these occasions she would invite other family members and friends, and the house would be filled.

One night a man by the name of Santiago James came home very tired. His wife, Ruth, served the evening meal, and after family worship they talked over the experiences of the day. She told him about her activities at home, and he told her about his work contacting people to offer them Christian books and the opportunities he had had to speak with people about the love of Jesus. Afterward Santiago went to bed and fell asleep, for the day had been long and tiring. Then he had an impressive dream in which he heard the voice of an angel. He woke up troubled, but soon went back to sleep. Then the same dream came to him once more. Just before daybreak it came again for a third time. In the dream Santiago found himself on a road that went through this city cemetery and afterward came to a crossroads. On the right he saw a house close to the sea, and over this house a bright light was shining. On the road that went to the left he saw, after passing two other houses, a third house, and over this house there was a light that was not quite as bright as the first one. And the angel said to him, "In the house that is close to the sea lives a widow who has 12 children; go and take her the message of salvation."

Santiago was powerfully impressed by the dream. He called his wife and told her about it. She encouraged him to go at once to where God was sending him. "Yes, I will go as soon as possible," he answered.

After breakfast and morning worship Santiago went to a quiet place where he could pray alone. He felt a great need for strength and courage to face the challenges of this new day. As he prayed he seemed to hear once again that voice that by now was familiar to him, and it said, "Go today; don't leave it for another day." Santiago gathered up his briefcase and materials, including his Bible. But before leaving, he asked his wife to pray that he could find the house and fulfill the Lord's command.

Like Abraham, he went out without knowing where he was going. He had never before seen that road. He did not even know where the cemetery was, because he had come to Cienfuegos only recently. So he first asked how to get to the cemetery. As soon as he began to walk in that direction, chills ran through his body. There before his eyes he saw the path he had already seen in his dreams three times.

He soon came to the crossroads and, in obedience to the angel's instructions, he took the path to the right. He came to a house that was near the farm where my grandmother lived. There he asked about a house that was home to a widow with 12 children. "Ah, you mean DonaAna! Yes, you are on the right path; at the following farm you will see the house—it's close to the sea. It's the only one there." Santiago felt his hair stand on end as he once again received confirmation that his dream had been from God. At once he continued on his way.

By this time it was midday. In Grandmother's house they had already set the table and were about to eat, when suddenly one of the boys exclaimed: "Mother, Mother! Here comes a man with a briefcase. Maybe he is a salesman."

"Bring a basin with clean water and a towel and put another plate on the table," ordered my grandmother. It was her custom to invite anyone who arrived at mealtime to eat with the family.

Santiago recognized the house as soon as he came near. It was just as he had seen it in the dream. He did not need to knock. To his amazement, the door opened. The family seemed to be expecting him. They invited him to come in, wash his hands, and sit at the table, something that had never happened before in his years as a colporteur. When he counted the number of sons and daughters at the table, he thought, *Didn't the angel tell me there were 12?* So he asked my grandmother about her other son or daughter who was missing.

"How did you know how many children I have? Yes, in fact, I have one more child, a daughter, who is married and has two children."

"Does she live on the opposite side of the crossroad?"

"Yes!" exclaimed Grandmother. "How did you know?"

Then Santiago told them about the dream and that God had sent him with a message for them.

When Santiago got out his Bible to share the Word with the family, my grandmother's joy intensified. "I want one!" she exclaimed with deep emotion. "Oh please, please, can you sell me your Bible." He said he would order a Bible for her and come back in a few days.

"That's fine," said Grandmother, "but in the meantime, you leave yours with me; I want to have a Bible today."

Seeing how interested my grandmother was in the Word of God, Santiago left his Bible with her, promising to return on Saturday so they could study together about the coming of Jesus and other truths.

That same night my grandmother began to read the Bible to her family, starting with Genesis. However, she was not satisfied with the chapters they read in their family gathering. The next morning, starting very early, she continued to read. Before long she came to chapter 20 in the book of Exodus. There she found the Ten Commandments and discovered what they say about the true day of rest. That night when the family came together, she read aloud Exodus 20. Then she added, "This is the law of God. Here it says the seventh day is the day of rest. From now on we will no longer work on Saturday."

The following day she continued to read, and in the third book,

Leviticus, she found the Bible instructions regarding clean and unclean foods. In the family gathering that night she said, "The Bible says that pigs are unclean. Tomorrow you will take that one that we have in the pen to the market and sell it. And we will never again eat pork or any other unclean animal here. And she read them the Bible instructions regarding clean and unclean meats.

So it was that every day they discovered the truths of the Bible, and they treasured them in their hearts, applying what they learned to practical life. How eager they were to learn all that God had written in His book!

On Friday morning my uncle Antonio, who took the farm products to market to sell and purchased the things that the family needed, came by our house. He told my mother about Santiago's visit and that Grandmother wanted us to come early on Saturday to hear what he had to say.

And my uncle added, "You know? Jesus will soon return to take us to heaven; it says so in the Bible. Tomorrow I will come for you in the car. Get the girls ready early."

After my uncle left, Mother called my sister and me. She told us what had happened. My sister was 7 years old, and I was only 5, but I still remember how my mother's face glowed with a joy I had never before seen in her. What we had read in *The Coming King* now seemed to be more real to her. Once again she reminded us of the nights she would go to the window looking toward heaven and ask, *How will He come? When will He come?* I also felt an immense joy knowing that Jesus would soon come back to earth.

On Saturday morning Brother Santiago came with Luis Mendoza, who could play the harmonica. These men were amazed at what they saw. They found my grandmother, her 12 children, and her two granddaughters all dressed in their best clothing. The house and the yards were clean, and there was no fire in the stove. On Friday the food had been prepared for Sabbath. My grandmother had thought about it and had concluded that the way to keep the Sabbath holy must be similar to the way they kept Good Friday when everything was prepared the day before, so that is what they had done. She also told them what they had read about clean and unclean animals and that they had sold the pig.

Santiago marveled at all of this. My grandmother asked him about images, and when he explained what the Bible taught about them, without hesitation she decided to tear down the altar and burn all of those images of the saints she had been venerating with such devotion.

Brother Luis played his harmonica while Santiago tried to teach us several hymns. That was our unforgettable first Sabbath school.

As we continued to study, our faith grew. Every night we met for worship at my grandmother's house and sang the hymns we had learned. Several of my uncles could play the guitar, and they accompanied the singing.

On the following Sabbaths, we met at 3:30 p.m., and Santiago came with Pastor Raul Miller and his family and a group of friends from the church at Cienfuegos. We children enjoyed our Sabbath school in the kitchen. There we learned beautiful children's songs that I still cherish in my memory.

After three months of study and preparation, the first baptism was conducted. That beautiful morning the pastor and all the members of the Cienfuegos church gathered at the beach, singing praises to God for His great love and mercy. Then my grandmother and the older children were baptized. The others were baptized as they became old enough.

The years have passed. My grandmother, my mother, and most of my aunts and uncles are resting now, waiting for the glorious resurrection morning. Those of us who are still alive look forward to the day we will join with them to sing the song of Moses and the Lamb. That is our joyful and glorious hope!

Chapter 17

Paths to Far Places

. . . .

Ruth Wheeler

Lo Wen-bi." Merritt Warren repeated the name aloud. He turned to his secretary. "Have we ever had a letter from anyone named Lo Wen-bi?"

The secretary looked up. "I've never heard the name before. Why do you ask?"

"Here is a most unusual letter. Its writer says Lo Wen-bi has been the leading Nosu preacher in the Ta Ting Mission for 10 years. I stopped at the Ta Ting Mission on my last trip, and he says he remembers my name and address from my calling card, which he took in to the mission director."

"Why does he write to you now?"

"Here, you can take the letter and read it aloud."

The secretary took the letter from the pastor. "A merchant in my village called to me one day. He said, 'Here are some papers called the *Signs of the Times*. They have to do with religion. I am a businessperson and have no time for religion. You are a preacher, and I think you might be interested in them.' I was, so I took them and read them. There was an article about the law of God, the Sabbath, and the change of the Sabbath. I see that the papers are sent from the same address as yours. Therefore, I am writing to you about this article. It does not teach the truth. It advises keeping the old Jewish Sabbath. I believe Christians should keep the Lord's Day, the day of His resurrection, the first day of the week, Sunday!"

Pastor Warren sensed that Mr. Lo was a sincere and honest man. He and his secretary knelt together and prayed that the Holy Spirit would help him to know just how to reply. Then he dictated an eight-page letter in which he tried to answer all of Mr. Lo's objections. He quoted the texts in full so as to be as clear as possible.

Thus began an earnest correspondence that lasted for more than two years between the missionary and the seeker for truth. Mr. Lo accepted the Bible truths as they were presented. He wrote to the pastor, requesting a visit. The missionary wrote back that he very much wanted to visit Mr. Lo and that he would do so as soon as he could.

Mr. Lo, who had taken the Christian name of Abraham, lived in Guizhou, a province Pastor Warren planned to revisit.

Three fourths of the inhabitants of Guizhou were of the Nosu race. Very few among the Nosu had any knowledge of the Bible and its teachings, and the missionary had a great burden to carry the message of the Savior to these people. The Warrens had made it a special part of their daily prayers that the way would open.

When a Chinese worker told them of a family named Yang, members of the Miao tribe, who wanted to learn Adventist beliefs, Merritt resolved to visit the faraway province. After some correspondence Mr. Yang invited the missionary to his home near Kiensi. Since Abraham Lo lived in the same part of Guizhou, the missionary wrote to this friend, offering to visit him also.

The trip into Guizhou proved a difficult one. No roads, not even a regular trail, penetrated the mountains in those days before the modernization of China. When he and Wang An-hsi, the Chinese pastor who accompanied him, reached Kiensi, they found Mr. Yang and conducted meetings in his home. However, the trip proved disappointing, for Yang and his family had little interest in what they taught. Feeling sad and depressed, the missionary and his helpers started for Ta Ting. As they walked along, they prayed aloud that God would in some way reach those mountain people. They had thought this visit would be an entering wedge, but somehow it had failed.

When he and his helpers reached Ta Ting, they found an inn and settled in for the night. Before they could go to bed, the innkeeper entered. "Is anyone here by the name of Wang Ho-ren? A man is looking for Wang Ho-ren."

"That's my name," Pastor Warren answered. (Wang Ho-ren was his name in Chinese.) Out on the street he met the inquirer, an aged man with a long white beard and a staff in his hand. He reminded the missionary of Bible pictures of the patriarch Jacob. With him was a younger man, his son.

"Is this Pastor Wang Ho-ren?" the old man asked. "I am Lo Wen-bi."

He dropped to his knees before the pastor and bowed his head.

"Stand up, brother. Stand up," the pastor urged. "You must not do that. We are brothers."

Lo Wen-bi and his son visited at length with the missionaries. The old man told of his conversion. He said he loved the people in the Ta Ting Mission, for they had brought him out of paganism and had taught him to love God and the Ten Commandments. But after reading the *Signs of the Times* and corresponding with Pastor Warren, he had received a new vision of what it meant to keep God's law.

When he began to keep the Sabbath, the people at the mission tried to dissuade him. He asked them to show him one text for Sundaykeeping, but they could not. They told him he could keep the Sabbath and continue working for them, but he should stay in his room on Saturday. However, Mr. Lo talked to everyone he met about God's commandments and how they should be kept.

Finally the mission director at Ta Ting arranged for an English missionary to spend a week studying Galatians with his group. At the end of the studies he said, "Abraham [Lo Wen-bi's Christian name], we want you to keep the Lord's Day. Saturday is the Jewish Sabbath, and Christians should keep the Lord's Day. You are not under the law but under grace. Therefore, you must take your stand and keep Sunday or be dismissed from our mission. We love you. You have been a faithful worker, but you must renounce the Jewish Sabbath. You must burn your Sabbath books."

Abraham Lo turned to Pastor Warren. "I told the mission director I did not want to do this, but if they insisted, I would. I said, 'I find nothing contrary to the Bible in those books, and I have one request to make.' I turned to the Law of God that hung behind the rostrum. I said, 'During the 10 years I have preached, I have often taken my text from that law. If you will tear that down and start the fire, I will put these books in it and let the fire burn them up.'"

Of course, the minister would not agree to this, and Abraham Lo and his eldest son were dismissed. "I went home to my farm high in the mountains," he said, "and that is where I am now."

The men visited far into the night. The hour grew so late that the missionary arranged for his guests to spend the remainder of the night in the hotel room next to the one he and Wang An-hsi, occupied. Early in the morning while it was still dark, Pastor Warren was awakened by someone speaking. Listening carefully, he could distinguish words. It was Abraham Lo talking to God. It did not sound like praying, but like a man talking to a friend.

Later that morning Pastor Warren asked Wang An-hsi if he had heard Abraham Lo pray during the night.

"Oh, yes," he replied. "The tears ran down my cheeks as I lay in bed. I've never heard anyone talk to God like that before."

Abraham Lo took the missionaries to his home out in the country. There he asked his son to bring "the bag." *Is it food?* Pastor Warren wondered. Abraham poured the contents on the table—copper coins, silver coins, and chunks of raw silver. "This," he said reverently, "is one tenth of our income since you sent me that tract about tithe paying. We don't know what to do with it. Is it all right for me to give it to you?"

In a voice choked with emotion Pastor Warren replied, "Yes, you may give it to me. I'll take it to Chungking [Chongqing] and turn it over to the mission treasurer. It will be used in the Lord's work. That will be paying it to the Lord."

"Thank you, brother. I want the Lord to have this."

Pastor Warren baptized Abraham, his wife, and their two sons in a mountain stream. When he and Wang left, they took the Lo family's younger son with them so he could train to be an evangelist.

Pastor Warren would have glad news to tell his wife. His and Wilma's prayers had been answered, for the Lo family belonged to the Nosu race. At last there were Nosu Seventh-day Adventists.

There would be others, many others, for Abraham shared his faith with his neighbors. Day by day he taught the people he met, and many came to know and love the God of heaven. The message continued to spread from village to village, far back into the mountains.

Chapter 18

A Floor to Kneel On

. . . .

John Baerg

One night when the moon was full, Sinival, a 16-year-old young man, came to our house in Fortaleza, Brazil, wanting to talk to a young woman of about the same age who lived with us and helped my wife with the housework. Her name was Olgarina.

Sinival got there early, and Olgarina had not yet finished her work. So he and I talked for a while in the living room.

First he asked me, "Do you remember the opening night of the meetings you held in the *pai do campo* neighborhood?"

I assured him that I remembered everything about that night.

"Allow me to tell you something you don't know yet. Four of us boys from the neighborhood saw the advertisements for the meetings and we decided to go and make a big ruckus and have some fun. But when we got there, everything was different from what we expected. We were met at the door by four well-dressed men. We looked inside and saw everything in order and attractively arranged. On one side there was a piano and beside it the Brazilian flag. So we went in quietly and sat down on the last bench. Our plan was to wait until everyone started to dance and shout and then we would run down the aisle screaming and shouting louder than anyone else to cause a disturbance.

"But that time never came. The meeting went on in perfect order. We heard soft music from the piano, and on the screen we saw a picture of Mary with Baby Jesus in her arms. It seemed to me the most beautiful picture I had ever seen, and then you began to tell us this story of Jesus and His great love for us. After a little while one of my friends said, 'This is not the kind of meeting we expected. Come on, let's go!'

"But I stayed there as if I were glued to the bench while my friends kept urging me to get up and go with them. Finally I told them, 'Go ahead if you want to. But leave me alone; I want to hear this.'"

Then Sinival told me that he had attended night after night, until one night his mother asked him, "Sinival, do you have a girlfriend? Where are you going every night so clean and well dressed?"

When he told his mother he was attending some meetings in *pai do campo*, she was horrified.

"Son, don't you know those are Protestant meetings?"

"No, I don't know that," Sinival answered. "But they don't attack anyone, and they never say anything bad about other religions. Instead, they tell us about Jesus, and they teach us that He wants to be our friend."

His mother had emphatically forbidden him to go again, but Sinival answered, "OK, Mother. Let's make a deal. You'll come with me just once, and if you don't like it, I will stop going too."

Horrified, his mother threw up her arms exclaiming, "Ave Maria! God save me from such a thing!"

Before long Sinival had a Bible of his own and a hymnal, and he began to attend church on Sabbath. His shirt was worn, but it was always clean and neatly pressed.

One day we made an announcement from the platform inviting all those who would like to belong to the choir that my wife, Coral, was organizing to come forward after the service. Somewhat timidly Sinival asked if he could join. My wife asked if he had a necktie. When he heard that, his hopes fell, but she immediately added, "Don't worry. My husband can give you one."

That night when Sinival came to talk with Olgarina, he had been singing in the choir for some time. As we spoke he asked me when he could be baptized. He was eager to formally belong to the church. Naturally that was the question I had been hoping for, and I joyfully told him that he could be baptized very soon.

One Friday, a few days later, I went to Sinival's home to speak with his mother. He had told me she was decidedly opposed to our religion, so I did not know how she would receive me. I found her washing clothes.

"Good morning, Dona Januaria," I said in greeting. "How are you?"

She was courteous. She apologized that her house was not as neat as she wished. When I said I was the professor in charge of the meetings in *pai do campo*, she said she figured as much because Sinival could talk of nothing else.

"I have come to speak with you about Sinival," I told her.

She seemed very concerned. "Has he done something wrong? Is he in trouble again?"

"No," I told her, "on the contrary. Your son has a great desire to do something very good. He wants to be baptized the way that the Lord Jesus was baptized."

"What do you mean by that?" she asked.

"As you know, 'baptize' is an ancient word that means to put something for an instant in the water."

"In the water!" exclaimed Dona Januaria, a bit alarmed.

"Yes, because it symbolizes the burial of the old life, the life we leave behind when we begin to follow Jesus. And when we come up out of the water, we are representing the resurrection and the beginning of a new spiritual life. The apostle Paul talks about this in Romans 6."

"Well, I'll be frank with you," said Dona Januaria. "The truth is that Sinival is very, very changed."

She shook her head, and from the expression on her face you would think her son had turned into a criminal. I asked somewhat fearfully, "Is he worse or better than before?"

"He is not just better, he is *much* better. He has stopped smoking and drinking; he doesn't gamble away his money or run around with his old gang. And—I can hardly believe it—but every penny of what he earns in the market he brings to me except what he calls tithes and offerings, which he takes to church."

Sinival had told me that his mother had been opposed when he began to keep the Sabbath, but when he had come home with two tithe envelopes, she had really been opposed.

He said, "Mother, see this? It's my name, Sinival Macedo. The teacher wrote my name on these two envelopes with his typewriter. One Sabbath I will take my tithe in this envelope and the next they will give me a receipt for the amount I turned in the week before. And it says here on the envelope that God will open the windows of heaven for all who are faithful in returning the part that belongs to Him. That is from the Bible, Mother. It's in Malachi 3:10."

"Malachi nothing!" she replied very angrily. "I can't believe how they have brainedwashed you."

Dona Januaria then reminded her son that there was no father in the home and that as the eldest he had to assume a greater responsibility. It was bad enough that he was resting on Saturday, when the rest of the family had to work, but it was even worse that he was planning to give the tenth part of his income to his new church.

Sinival had told me about this conversation, but now that I was face to face with his mother, it was evident that a lot had changed. After talking with her for a while, I asked her approval to baptize her son. She immediately replied, "If that is what he wants, he can do it; now he is a good son."

Then I told her that she should be present for such an important ceremony and that it would be good if she started attending the next day so she could get accustomed to coming. She didn't promise, but before leaving, I said, "Let's kneel. I want to pray for your home and especially for you and Sinival."

She wouldn't allow me to kneel until she had spread out a clean cloth on the floor.

That afternoon Dona Januaria met someone on the street who was a member of our church and said to her, "Guess who visited me this morning? The professor himself came in person. And he invited me to church. What shall I do? I don't have any clothes for that."

The sister replied, "If the teacher, who is such a busy person, took the time to visit you in person, you should come."

And she did come. She sat in my Sabbath school class. I introduced her as Sinival's mother, and everyone greeted her. They were very happy to see her.

She liked the program that day, and from then on she never missed a meeting. Two months later she told me she too wanted to be baptized. Her daughter also surrendered her heart to the Lord, and a year later so did her other son. Now it was a united and happy family.

Several months later Sinival came to my house to talk about something very important. I could tell he was not as relaxed and casual as he usually was when he came to talk with Olgarina.

"Pastor, could you lend me 150 cruzeiros until next Tuesday?" he asked.

I wanted to know why he needed the money. "To finish putting a roof on our house."

"Oh, you are changing the roof?"

"No, Pastor, we are building a new house, and right now we are lacking only 150 cruzeiros to finish the roof.

I gladly let him have the money.

On the appointed day Sinival came and returned the money he had borrowed and asked if I would be free the following Thursday at 4:00 p.m. I told him I would be.

"Then could you come and dedicate our house?"

"Of course."

That Thursday afternoon I had a great surprise. Instead of a house that looked like any breeze might blow it over, instead of a house in which the doors and windows didn't fit because they were twisted and warped, instead of a dirty floor that was filled with holes, there was a completely new house. The doors and windows were all painted with bright colors. The floor was new, clean, and polished. A little table in the living room was covered with a beautiful cloth, and there was a vase of fresh-cut flowers next to a Bible and a hymnal. Several neighbors were there, all dressed for the occasion. When the family and the visitors were seated, I asked Dona Januaria what she wanted me to do. She asked that we sing a hymn. Then she asked me to read something from the Bible.

I read Isaiah 65, which describes our home in the new earth. Then I asked, "Now shall we have the prayer of dedication?"

"Yes," she said. "Now we have a floor to kneel on."

She had resolved, that Friday when I visited her the first time, that one day she would have a house with a floor so clean that anyone could kneel on it. And that day had come.

After the prayer, while she prepared to serve us some food, I asked the happy woman, "Sister Januaria, tell me something. You used to work seven days and never rest. You spent all your money without returning any of it as tithes and offerings or helping the poor. In spite of that, you hardly had enough means even for food, and you were ashamed of the clothing you wore. Now you work only six days, you tithe faithfully and give offerings. You spend money on the bus to go to the meetings and choir practice and missionary journeys. Nevertheless, you have new clothes, and I see your face is healthy and well nourished. How do you explain it?"

With a beautiful smile Sister Januaria raised her arms and said, "Pastor, in this house no one needs to ask how we can explain it. Here the blessings of God are so abundant you can see them from miles around." When she said that, she and everyone else laughed heartily.

I will never forget Sister Januaria. Now she is resting in the Lord, but her memory lingers on.

When my wife and I left Brazil not long ago, our ship stopped for 24 hours in Belem. We ate with Sinival and Olgarina in their two-story home. Sinival is the owner of a taxi, and their children are beautiful and intelligent. I have no idea why we all cried when we had prayer before leaving. There was really nothing to cry about, was there?

Chapter 19

Sometimes Change
Is Like an Earthquake

. . . .
Alcyon Fleck

The receptionist in the offices of the Adventist mission in Guatemala City was bent over the work on her desk one day when someone came in. When she raised her eyes to greet the visitor, she saw that it was a priest.

"Good morning. What can we do for you?" she asked courteously.

"May I speak with Señor Fleck, *por favor*?" the visitor asked. "I believe he is the leader of your church here in Guatemala; is that right?"

"Yes, he is; but unfortunately, Pastor Fleck left a few minutes ago. We expect him back this afternoon around 2:00, Raquel answered. "Would you care to leave a message?"

The priest was visibly disappointed. After a brief hesitation he said, "Very well, I'll leave the address where I can be found in this city. Will you please ask him to call on me at his earliest convenience?"

"Yes, of course I will give your message to Pastor Fleck," the secretary assured.

When the president arrived at the office shortly before 2:00, Raquel said, "Pastor, we had a visitor this morning. A priest came here looking for you. He left his name and address and asked that you call on him." Raquel handed him the card the priest had left.

"H'mmm. It says his name is Rafael González; I think I'll see him at once."

Pastor Fleck located the street that was on the slip of paper and began looking for the house number. Finally, he discovered that the number he was looking for was above the door of a large Catholic church.

He entered and inquired of the first person he met for "Padre Rafael González." The young man said he would call the padre.

As Pastor Fleck stood waiting, he looked around him. "What a gorgeous church!" he said half aloud. His thoughts were interrupted when a man about his own age stood before him. Pastor Fleck was impressed with the honest, clean-cut face.

"Señor Fleck?" the young priest asked, extending his hand.

"Yes; and you must be Rafael González."

"Thank you for coming, Señor Fleck. I have been very anxious to meet you," the priest said eagerly.

"I am glad if I can be of service," replied the mission president.

After looking around to be sure that no one was listening, Rafael explained in a soft voice, "Someone gave me several Adventist books. I have read them, and now I have many questions in my mind. I was told you could help me."

"I'll be glad to do anything I can. What if you came to my office, where we can talk privately?"

"You are right," replied the priest, breathing easier. "I will meet you there in a little while."

Behind the closed door of Pastor Fleck's office the priest and the missionary began their conversation.

"I am curious to know how you became interested in these things. You must know this is unusual," said the president.

"Yes, I suppose it is," Rafael answered. "Actually, it started one evening when I was at a family gathering with one of my parishioners. There I was introduced to a member of your church, Herminia de Sosa. Maybe you know her."

"Yes, she is an outstanding person. Always cheerful and optimistic."

"I spoke with her briefly, and she gave me a copy of *El Centinela* magazine. I accepted, planning to burn it as soon as possible. However, while I was carrying the magazine toward the trash, an article caught my eye. It was about the second coming of Christ. By the time I finally burned the paper, I had read it all.

"Several days later," he continued, "I met this woman again. This time she was with her mother, Señora Martinez, and the older woman said something that really set me to thinking. She said I wasn't keeping the Ten Commandments. The truth is that her words provoked me a lot."

"Of course," said Pastor Fleck, "that's understandable."

"So, quite irritated, I said to her, 'And which of the commandments do you imagine I am not keeping?' I thought the old women in the parish must be making up some scandal about me."

Pastor Fleck laughed and said, "It's true that some people seem to entertain themselves by bearing false witness."

"'Well,' Mrs. Martínez said, 'what if we get your Bible and read the commandments so that you can see for yourself if it is true what I am saying.'

"So I brought my own Bible, and she opened it to Exodus 20. After reading the second commandment, which talks about images, she stopped and said, 'You break this one every day.'

" 'You are mistaken,' I replied. 'We do not worship the images. We simply venerate them. They are like portraits that make the saints more vivid in our minds.'

"In reply, she read the text again, and said to me, 'As you can see, Father, the commandment is specific and categorical. It does not simply forbid us to "worship" images. It says, "You shall not bow down to them, nor honor them." Do you sincerely believe that you are in full obedience to this commandment?'

"With that, she had touched a sensitive point," said the priest. "I have always tried to be sincere. I long to serve God and do His will. So I didn't answer at the moment, but, as a matter of fact, I had already noticed those words in the commandment, and I had no answer; so I decided it would be better to say nothing. I asked her, 'And what else do you want to tell me?'

"Then she read the fourth commandment, which says, 'Remember that thou keep holy the Sabbath day. Six days shalt thou labour, and shalt do all thy works. But the seventh day is the Sabbath of the Lord thy God: thou shalt do no work on it.' And she said to me, 'You're not keeping that commandment, either, unless you are resting on Saturday.'

"Of course, I did not accept or believe at that moment that the woman could be right. It seemed to me that there must be some logical explanation, even though I didn't have one right at the moment. So as a result I felt the urgent need to clarify these things."

"So you decided to come here with your questions?" asked Pastor Fleck.

"Well, not really, because this happened some months ago. The decision I made at that time was to dedicate myself to studying the Bible as never before. I thought that the answer must be there somewhere."

"An excellent decision! So you began studying the Bible."

"Day and night."

"And with that, things have cleared up for you?"

"The more I study, the more confused I have become."

"How is that possible? Do you think the Bible is not clear in what it teaches about these things?"

"That is precisely the problem. It is altogether too clear. The confusion comes when I compare the teachings of Scripture with what I have been practicing all my life. I am overwhelmed by feelings of guilt. I have an internal conflict and can't seem to find a solution."

As the two men continued to talk, Pastor Fleck was surprised to find that the young priest had a clear understanding of the principal teachings of Scripture. He was even convinced of the need to observe the seventh-day Sabbath. He had read the book *Steps to Christ* and other works by Ellen White, and he believed that she was in some way inspired by God. However, concerning our state in death, he was still greatly perplexed.

"I understand that you teach that people lose consciousness when they die and sleep until the time of the resurrection. That I cannot understand, and it seems to me it would be very difficult to accept."

"But you already have the key in your hands. The important thing to ask is not What does this group or that person teach about it? but What does the Bible say? If you are honest with God and pray for understanding, His Spirit will illuminate your mind with the truths from His Word."

Rafael was silent for a long moment, and finally, with a deep sigh, he said, "Please pray for me, Pastor. I must find peace of mind. My most earnest desire is that God will show me the truth. I cannot possibly imagine any course apart from the priesthood, to which I dedicated my life in childhood. In fact, to think of leaving it fills me with dread and fear; but God knows my heart. My sincere desire is to follow where He leads." An expression of tension and worry was written on his face as he spoke.

"God's love for His children is beyond our comprehension," said the pastor.

"I am completely convinced of that."

"This point may not be completely clear for you right now, but you have put your trust in God. I encourage you to continue studying the Word and praying. Ask for divine guidance every day."

Selecting some books from his library, the missionary handed them to the priest, saying, "Perhaps these will be of some help to you as you study further. Remember, we are ready to help you in any way we can. We'll be praying for you."

Rafael returned to his parish with a heavy heart. During his conversation with Pastor Fleck, the way ahead did not look too hard for him. But when he found himself alone, clouds of doubt crowded in upon him.

Every spare moment Rafael spent studying the Bible. The sacredness of the seventh-day Sabbath had been clear to him almost from the beginning, and he was convicted that he must find a way to keep it. He no longer believed in confession to a priest or in bowing down to saints, although he was forced by circumstances to carry on such activities in his church. He modified the order of his services. Candles were used less and less in the church, and he admonished his congregation to study the Bible. The material in *Steps to Christ* was used more and more in his Sunday sermons.

But when he considered the subject of the state of the dead, Rafael continued to be puzzled. *How can I believe such a materialistic theory?* he thought. *If it weren't for some of these texts in the Bible, I would just forget it.*

A few months later Pastor Fleck was again surprised by a visit from Padre Rafael. "Come in!" the pastor greeted him warmly. "I am so glad to see you."

In the privacy of the pastor's office Rafael immediately began a discussion of the doctrines he had been studying. "Pastor Fleck, I have read all the books you gave me. And I have read and studied many other things on the subject, but I seem unable to accept the doctrine of human unconsciousness in death."

"I am sure it is not easy to change ideas you have held all your life," the pastor replied. "However, it is not our ideas that count; God's Word is the only safe guide. How do you understand the teaching of Ecclesiastes 9:5, 6, where it says, 'The living know that they shall die: but the dead know not any thing'?"

"Yes, I know about that passage, and it is clear, but that is from the Old Testament. Christ had not yet come at that time."

"Have you thought about 1 Timothy 6:14-16, where it says that only God has immortality?"

"If only God has immortality," said Rafael, "then what about the redeemed? Do they just die and that's the end of everything?"

"Of course not. In 1 Corinthians 15:51-53 it says, 'Behold, I show you a mystery; We shall not all sleep, but we shall all be changed, in a moment, in the twinkling of an eye, at the last trump: for the trumpet shall sound, and the dead shall be raised incorruptible.' It is talking here about the Second Coming, isn't it?"

"Yes, of course. It is talking about the resurrection of the just."

"Now, notice the words that follow: 'We shall be changed, for this corruptible must put on incorruption, and this mortal must put on immortality.' It says clearly that human beings will be clothed with immortality when Christ returns."

"It says that, but I don't know. Maybe it means that at that time we will receive some kind of higher immortality than we had before."

"Wouldn't it be preferable to simply accept what the text says?"

Rafael did not answer, but his face reflected a deep inner struggle.

"Look, maybe it will help you understand the matter if I ask you something else," said Pastor Fleck. "I'm sure you remember the Apostles' Creed. What does it say?"

"The Creed? Mmmm, . . . it says, 'I believe in God, the Father almighty, creator of heaven and earth. I believe in Jesus Christ, His only Son, our Lord. He was conceived by the power of the Holy Spirit and born of the Virgin Mary. He suffered under Pontius Pilate, was crucified, died, and was buried. On the third day he rose again. He ascended into heaven and is seated at the right hand of the Father. He will come again to judge the living and the dead.'"

"Notice the words 'He will come again.' That's talking about the Second Coming, isn't it?"

"Of course, but what does that have to do with . . . ?"

"Well, after He judges the living and the dead, what will He do then?"

"Then He will give them their reward, whatever they deserve."

"What is this 'reward'?"

"Well, then the righteous will receive eternal life and the . . . "

There Rafael stopped, and his face grew red because his mind had caught the implication of what he was saying.

Pastor Fleck added, "That means that before we are judged, and before the second coming of Christ, no one will receive eternal life and no one will be punished for his or her sins. This couldn't happen the instant we die, because the judgment does not take place until the Second Coming. Don't you agree?"

There was a long silence. Finally the priest said, "I don't know. I understand what you say, but it is so hard."

This time Rafael went back to his parish even more deeply discouraged and disillusioned. He realized that he had gone to the Adventist pastor to vindicate his own ideas rather than to receive help. He had been surprised at the texts the pastor could find to answer his arguments. Again and again he asked himself, *How can I admit that what I have always believed is wrong?*

Señora Martinez and her husband continued writing to Rafael, encouraging him to study and search for truth. Lengthy discussions took place in letters between the couple and the priest. As the weeks went by, Rafael realized that one by one his former ideas were being replaced by the truth from the Holy Scriptures.

At last he was convinced of the Bible truth concerning the soul and human condition in death. If he wanted to be faithful to the teachings of Scripture, he would have to admit that it is not until Jesus comes again that "this corruptible is clothed with incorruption" and human beings will receive immortality.

When he understood this, the rituals, the masses for the dead, and the prayers to the saints became meaningless. Now he seemed to be caught in an unsolvable dilemma. He now believed the Bible doctrines, but to change his way of life, to leave the only thing that was familiar to him, seemed unthinkable. Some days he almost convinced himself that he should forget everything He had learned and return to the same old pattern. Surely the Lord would accept his life of sacrifice. Yet when he read his Bible, he knew he could not go on teaching and practicing things he did not believe.

At this crucial time Rafael decided to spend 10 days in special spiritual exercises and to settle this problem once and for all. He saw no one during this period and ate very little food. He put the Bible and the Adventist literature on one side and the books of doctrine and tradition from his church on the other. Reading first one and then the other, he compared them point by point. While reading the doctrines of the Roman Catholic Church, he felt burdened, perplexed, and unhappy; but when he turned to the Bible, the weight lifted from his heart.

At the end of the 10 days Rafael felt constrained to go to a friend, an older priest, to make confession.

"You say you have been reading Protestant propaganda?" questioned the white-haired man.

"Yes, Father, I have. But that isn't the worst; I believe it."

"Alas, my son!" exclaimed the old man. "You have made a great mistake. What prompted you to do such a thing?"

"Well, Father, it is this way," Rafael explained. "For some time I have been concerned over the differences between the doctrines of the church and the Holy Scriptures. My mind has been plagued with doubts for months. Have you never had doubts, Father?"

"Of course, everyone has doubts," said the older man. "But I decided years ago to put such thoughts out of my mind. After all, the mother church is the final authority. I leave such things up to her."

The elderly priest felt he had solved the problem for the younger, less-experienced man. "After all," he said, "there are some things that can't be explained."

Rafael took his leave courteously from his friend, but he was far from satisfied. *He may leave his conscience in the hands of the church; but I know I'll have to answer for myself. This is between me and God. With His help I'll find the answer.*

From then on Rafael knew in his heart that he must leave the priesthood; he couldn't live a lie. It was more and more difficult for him to preach with sincerity and to perform the rites of the church.

"But these people!" he asked himself again and again. "All these people in my parish! They have such confidence in me. What will become of them if I leave?"

To leave the priesthood secretly seemed unthinkable. "I must pray that God will help me find a way to make this change in my life."

The tremendous struggle continued in Rafael's heart. His mind was never at rest, and many times he found himself unable to sleep at night because of his perplexity. Every day he prayed, "Lord, help me find the way. Give me an opportunity. Open a door for me through the impenetrable wall that I face. Most of all, give me the courage and strength to follow Thy leading."

Then one day a letter arrived from the superior. "Now, what can this be about?" Rafael asked himself as he looked through his mail. Tearing open the envelope, he read: "You may make plans to take a vacation in Mexico. You will leave for Guatemala City, Wednesday, October 15. In the capital you can arrange your passport and other papers."

This was a surprise for Rafael, for he had received no previous word of an upcoming vacation. However, the prospect of a few weeks in Mexico was pleasant. One of his mother's sisters lived in Mexico City, and he would enjoy visiting her.

Rafael made all necessary arrangements for the church services to be conducted properly in his absence, and on the afternoon of October 15 he boarded the old bus that seemed to be overflowing with humanity, baggage, and chickens. At the next village Rafael got off, planning to board the night train for Guatemala City. He arrived in good time at the station and was about to buy his ticket when he saw three familiar faces, one of them his superior. Two other priests were with the stern-faced cleric.

"Father Rafael, we have been waiting for you," the superior said.

"I am here at your orders," replied Rafael. "I was told to make preparations for a vacation in Mexico, and that is what I have done."

"We are here to inform you that you are under suspicion of showing sympathy to these Protestant devils and of giving them money."

Rafael's usual good nature vanished, and he felt his face turn red. "It is true that I have donated to people carrying on welfare and missionary work. This is a worthy cause that I can testify to from personal observation during my many years as a missionary in China. As for their being Protestant devils, I have found nothing about their work or deportment that could possibly class them as devils."

You Won't Be Needing This

Being in a public place, the superior would not lower his dignity to carry the point further. He said, "Apparently you are already well contaminated by these sons of Luther. You are not leaving for a trip to Mexico; rather, you are being expelled to another country to see if you will repent and forget this heresy. You are to report to the rectory in Guatemala City. There you will arrange your papers and go to El Salvador."

While Rafael stood stunned and dumbfounded, one of the three priests ordered him to open his suitcase for their inspection, no doubt looking for Protestant propaganda. In this the zealot was disappointed. But he took out a good suit that Rafael had recently purchased, with the remark "You won't be needing this."

As Rafael looked for a seat on the train, he felt his face still burning with the sting of the words and the rough treatment he had received. This was the thanks he had received for all his years of service! He had given the best years of his life, and never in all these years had he received a salary, only a stipend for his bare necessities. He sat staring out the window, oblivious to everything except his own thoughts. He hardly noticed when the train started, even though there had been the usual bustle of departure.

As the train rolled through the country, Rafael's thinking began to clear. Could this be the answer to his prayer? He had asked God for the opportunity to follow his convictions. It seemed incredible that it should be brought about by this unexpected turn of events. He had prayed for God to show him the way. Now the answer seemed evident. Was he really going to make this tremendous change in his life?

If I renounce my faith and my present position, break my connections, and lose all the security I have known, what then? Pastor Fleck has never promised me anything more than the assurance that God will provide a way.

When I arrive in Guatemala City, I will not go to the rectory, he said to himself. *I will go to the mission office, find Pastor Fleck, and tell him of my decision. I feel sure he will know what I should do. But what if Pastor Fleck is not there? I know he sometimes goes on trips that take him out of the city for days.*

This last thought brought alarm to Rafael. Now that his decision had been made, he must have everything settled soon. *Lord,* he prayed, *it may seem like asking a lot, but please let the pastor be there.*

Rafael now felt happier than he had for months. His heart was placed in God's hand. *It does not matter what the future holds,* he reminded himself. *If I can feel the warmth of God's approving smile, I am sure that life will hold nothing too hard for me.*

"Well, Padre Rafael! How are you? You must be very happy tonight. I notice you are singing." It was one of Rafael's parishioners speaking.

"Pedro! I am glad to see you. Yes, I am happy tonight," Rafael answered without divulging his thoughts.

As the train approached the city at dawn, Rafael was troubled by a new thought. *Maybe they are expecting me at the rectory. What if they have sent someone to meet me at the station?*

It would be better, he decided, to leave the train at the small station at the edge of town and avoid the possibility of further complications. When the train stopped, Rafael and several other passengers got off. He hailed a taxi and went to a small hotel near the mission office. It was a strange feeling, this new independence!

Rafael was disappointed when he arrived at the office later in the morning to find that Pastor Fleck was not in. However, he was relieved to know that the president would be in the office that afternoon.

In the afternoon he returned to the mission office. "Good afternoon, señorita. Has the pastor arrived yet?" Rafael asked the young woman at the reception desk.

"Oh, yes," she smiled. "Pastor Fleck is here, and he is expecting you." As he followed the secretary to the inner office, Rafael made a mental note: *Even the secretaries here radiate a Christian atmosphere.*

"Well, what a happy surprise!" Pastor Fleck greeted the priest warmly.

Reassured by the cordial welcome from the missionary, Rafael plunged immediately into the real purpose of his visit. "Pastor Fleck, I have been so anxious to see you. This time I have come to tell you of my decision."

Pastor Fleck listened, studying the expression of the man intently. "What decision have you made, my friend? Tell me about it."

"Pastor, since I saw you several months ago, I have been going through a crisis. I advanced every possible argument to excuse myself from the obligation of accepting this new doctrine, but it hasn't worked. My mind returned again and again to the same points, and I have finally recognized that it is all founded on the Bible. Today I have come to tell you that if you believe my sincerity and will accept me, I would consider it the highest privilege to be considered a brother of yours in the faith. From this day forth, with God's help, it is my sincere desire and determination to be a Seventh-day Adventist."

For a moment the Adventist pastor was without words to express the thrill and joy that welled up in his heart. He thought, *This is the greatest miracle I could ever hope to see.* Aloud he said, "Brother González, this is wonderful! Please tell me the whole story."

Rafael recounted his experience, going over the various points of doctrine that had been big hurdles for him. He told of the sleepless nights, the torment of spirit, the hours of doubt and despair, the endless searching and studying, the fear of an insecure future, and the awareness of what this decision would mean to his family.

Not having known Rafael personally or his background, the pastor felt it his responsibility to question him thoroughly in regard to his real motives for making this drastic change. There had been cases, he remembered, during which deception had been practiced.

However, there was little doubt in Pastor Fleck's mind as to the padre's sincerity or his character, for some of the Adventist members from the district in which Rafael had labored had reported their knowledge of the priest, and none of them had intimated anything against his good name. The pastor went over all the main points of doctrine and ascertained that the priest was fully convinced of their soundness.

After a long and intense conversation, Pastor Fleck asked, "And now, my brother, what are your plans?"

"Plans? I don't have any plans, Pastor. As you know, I am from Spain. I came here as a missionary. Now that God has turned me from my former plans and purposes, it seems that I must begin anew. How I am to do that, I do not understand as yet."

"I'm sure the future looks very uncertain right now, my friend. But you can be sure that God has a plan for your life," said the missionary. "If you completely dedicate your life and yourself to Him, He will show you the way. In the meantime, we stand ready to help you. You can count on us as your friends."

Before Rafael left the pastor's office, they knelt to pray. Rafael offered a sincere prayer of consecration and submission to God's will, a prayer of thankfulness to God for His Holy Spirit who had guided his life, illumined his mind, and transformed his heart.

After the prayer the missionary welcomed Rafael into the household of faith with the customary Latin embrace. Each noticed tears brimming in the eyes of his brother. Rafael left the mission office late that afternoon. *God is so good*, he said to himself. *I know with certainty that He has led me. I may not clearly see the future, but with Jesus at my side, I know it will be wonderful.*

At that critical moment Rafael González could not see into the future, but it was true, as Pastor Fleck had told him, that the Lord had beautiful plans for him, including the blessing of a happy home and a life of service in the pastoral ministry of the Seventh-day Adventist Church.

Chapter 20

Korean Caveman

. . . .

Theodora Wagnerin

Han Ho Sun had been drinking again. His black hair shone in the sunlight as he strolled aimlessly around the crowded marketplace in his hometown on Cheju Island. Nothing mattered much today. He had nothing to do, and he even had a little money left to jingle in his pocket.

"Good afternoon, sir. I have something here that will interest you," said a pleasant voice.

Han turned to find a man holding a magazine, the Korean *Signs of the Times*. It was for sale, the man said, and he named the price.

Sure, he'd buy a copy. Han reached into his pocket for a coin.

"I'm sure you would appreciate having this good magazine come to your home regularly," the man continued. He pointed out many of the attractive features and stated the price of a year's subscription.

Of course Han would take it for a year. Why not? Spending his money gave him a sense of importance, and he felt very jovial today.

That night Han slept the sleep of an intoxicated man. In the morning, when the alcohol had worn off, he found the magazine in his pocket and was extremely disgusted. "Whatever possessed me to buy a religious magazine? I have no more need of this than a dog has need for two tails!" He threw the magazine on the floor and stomped on it.

For a long time he sat at the table with his head in his hands, longing to be free from the headache he was suffering because of the effects of the alcohol.

At length, he opened his eyes again and saw the wrinkled magazine still on the floor. Again he was angry, but after a while he thought, *I've spent my money. I might as well see what it says.* So he reached over and picked up the paper. He tried to brush off the dirt and straighten it a bit, and then laboriously he began to read.

At first he understood almost nothing, but as he continued to read, his brain cleared up a bit, and he realized it was like nothing he had ever seen before. The articles told about a God who loves us and takes a personal interest in our lives. Han had heard of the Bible, but he never imagined he could find such practical and helpful ideas in its pages. By the time he had read the last article, a determination had sprung up in his heart to know the Bible teachings for himself.

Han knew that on the island a small group of Presbyterian believers met to worship God. So he sought them out and from then on rejoiced as he learned more about what it means to be a child of God.

As he came to know Jesus as a Friend and Savior, Han felt a joy he had never known before, and his heart overflowed with a desire to share all he was learning with his family. He did not doubt that they, too, would accept the message of salvation. But his father became angry and shouted, "Son, stay away from those Christians! Don't you know they are barbarians?" Fearful that their ancestral gods would be offended should this rebel son continue to pray to God, they soon turned him out.

As the monthly issues of the *Signs* magazine began to arrive, Han read every article three or four times, comparing its teaching with the Bible. In this way he soon discovered the truth about the Sabbath. At once he began to observe that day.

Filled with enthusiasm more than tact, he talked constantly about the Sabbath to the little group of Christians with whom he was worshipping. The church officers became agitated and told Han that if he would not quit talking about the Sabbath, he was no longer welcome to worship with them.

And so it was that Han found himself ostracized not only by his unbelieving family but also by the only Christians he knew. Sad and perplexed, he took his roll of bedding and his books and slowly climbed Mount Hallisan to make his home in a cave.

The cave became his sanctuary, a place for deep soul searching. Alone with God, he found strength in prayer. He also studied his Bible as days of solitude passed slowly. At night even deeper silence hung over the cave, but Han enjoyed heavenly companionship.

The place became his schoolroom, and the Lord his teacher. God saw in this young man qualifications that would make him a valuable Christian worker, but not until he had gained control of himself and learned to work in God's way.

One morning a Buddhist priest stopped at the entrance of the cave and stood transfixed as he listened to Han pray. When Han had finished, the priest said, "I have been in the habit of coming to this cave to meditate and pray to Buddha. I have seen Buddhist monks fingering their prayer beads and chanting the sutra. I have heard scores of priests praying and mumbling in a singsong fashion, but never have I heard anyone pray as you prayed. I believe you are in touch with the Majesty of heaven."

As Han endeavored to share his faith with the Buddhist, an interesting conversation followed. When the priest left, he said, "I will go down to the village and tell the people about you and your Savior."

The Buddhist kept his promise. He encouraged the villagers to go to the cave and talk with the man who was in touch with the Almighty, and people flocked to the cave and listened as Han told them about God, His loving-kindness, and the wonderful salvation provided by the Savior. A number of those who listened accepted Christianity. They invited Han to come to their village and preach.

In the fall of that year two Adventist missionaries, C. L. Butterfield and R. C. Wangerin, visited the island, baptized the converts, and organized a church. The new believers immediately began to teach others.

Han Ho Sun developed into an earnest Christian. But what he had learned was too good to keep to himself, so he became a literature evangelist. In summer's heat and winter's cold, with a pack of books on his back, he walked over narrow mountain trails and through valleys, searching for honest persons.

Although Han's educational advantages have been few, in the hands of God he has become a tool to bring many people their first knowledge of the gospel. In his vest pocket he carries a little black notebook containing the names of 150 individuals who have accepted Christ as their Savior through his personal efforts.

Chapter 21

God of the Unexpected

. . . .

Gilma Carbonell

I don't know how long the Lord was crouching by my path waiting to spring, but I do know that when it happened it was traumatic. Not only because it was so unexpected, but because it seemed like the last thing that would have been possible.

I was born in Guantánamo. This is the easternmost province of Cuba and the location of a famous U.S. naval base. My mother has a doctorate in education. She is a capable person with strong convictions about life and how to live it. Her views are deeply rooted in the ideals of Communism. She does not believe in God, and naturally she shared her convictions with me. I was convinced that Mother's viewpoint was completely logical, and it seemed that only a truly ignorant person could believe in God.

Like my mother, whom I greatly love and admire, I decided to become a teacher. I have always enjoyed research and wanted to look deeply into the roots of our convictions, so I specialized in the history and philosophy of Marxism. I made excellent grades, and after graduating began to work as a teacher in my home city of Los Maceo.

Teaching gave me a sense of satisfaction and fulfillment. I was happy, not only to be advancing professionally in my chosen field, but also because of the conviction that I was helping many young people come out of ignorance and find a better way of life.

This is not to imply that the Bible was an unknown book to me. I had purchased a copy, and I read it often with the purpose of finding its errors. And in fact, I found a lot of them. I began to underline all the absurd things in the Bible, and I used this as a teaching tool in my classes. All of this was to change in a way that was totally unexpected.

I had joined a circle of professionals in my city who met periodically to share the results of their investigations. I decided to undertake a research project about something that had always puzzled me. José Martí is a hero of the Cuban struggle for independence from Spain. Martí carried on his efforts not only in the field of politics and military strategy but also as a famous poet and writer.

What I found hard to understand was that Martí, in spite of being obviously intelligent, was a believer. Wanting to present a good paper to my research group, I set out to study everything he had written, especially on the subject of faith. As a result, I not only organized a paper that seemed worthwhile to me, but also, without actually realizing it, came to see that his view was defensible.

After reading my paper to the group, I was immediately attacked by the leaders, who accused me of defending the existence of God. Under their aggressive questioning, I did in fact defend this position, although I still considered myself a materialist. It must have been that even then God was helping me, because I have no idea where I came up with some of the thoughts I expressed that day.

But it was a devastating experience. I went home shattered. I couldn't believe what had happened. Had I actually defended the existence of God? *But I am an atheist! What have I done?* I closed all the windows and doors and fell on my knees. In tears, I cried out, "God, if you exist, I want to know you."

At that very instant I began to feel something strange in my being. Amazed, I picked up my marked Bible and began to turn its pages. As I did, it seemed as if a blindfold fell from my eyes. The things I had not understood suddenly began to make sense.

The days that followed were the strangest of my life. I had an insatiable hunger and thirst for knowledge of the Bible. Day and night I read it with intense rejoicing. I also began to review what I knew of mathematics, biology, and physics, and I became profoundly convicted that my former understanding of these areas was mistaken, because I had seen them as refuting the existence of God.

I began to wonder if I was losing my mind, because it seemed to me that something or Someone was guiding me at every step—I felt like a person who suddenly begins hearing voices and believes he or she must be going insane. I spoke with a Baptist pastor who explained to me about the Holy Spirit. He told me that God was calling me. I began to attend his church and rejoiced in the good preaching and Bible instruction I received there. I also attended services in other congregations in the city, taking advantage of every opportunity to learn more about the Scriptures.

One day as I was crossing the central plaza of Los Maceo, I saw a young man seated in a wheelchair. Some years ago I had had orthopedic surgery that left me unable to walk for two years, which is probably the reason I sympathize with people in this situation. I went over to talk with the boy.

I found him in a lighthearted mood. The conversation might not have gone much further, but at that point another young man came by, and the boy in the wheelchair introduced us, saying that his friend was a youth leader in their church. The second young man immediately invited me to attend, and he mentioned that they were Seventh-day Adventists. I was eager to hear anything that had to do with the Word of God, so I did not hesitate to accept his invitation, and on the following Saturday I was present at the Adventist church.

This is how I first came to hear about the Sabbath, and I was brought face to face with the question Which denomination is closest to the truth? It seemed to me that none of them could have it all, but there had to be one that was closer than the rest. As He had already done so many times before, the Lord now opened the door to my understanding through Scripture. I prayed fervently for guidance. Now it seemed that anywhere I opened the Bible there was another text that spoke about the Sabbath.

About this time Enrique Almenares, a church elder, began to study the Bible with me. He is a well-organized man and began to carefully show me the foundations of Scripture knowledge. But I was too impatient for his method. What I was finding in my own search was advancing rapidly, and in less than a month I told Brother Almenares that I wanted to be baptized.

Understandably, he was doubtful about this, but he agreed to take my name to the church board. Their answer was an emphatic no! I was well known in Los Maceo, and when the good people on the board heard of my quick decision, they were convinced that I must be a spy who had been coached by state security to apply for membership. The pastor himself came by to tell me about the board's decision. When he saw my reaction, he seemed thoughtful, and after a few minutes he said, "Gilma, we need to pray about this."

I don't know what the pastor did, but I know what I did: I prayed day and night. And the Lord heard, because the next time he took my name to the board, it was approved.

I had been an honors student during teacher training and had received numerous awards and privileges, but none of this made any difference at this point. I could no longer teach what I had always taught because I no longer believed what I had always believed. Very soon the school authorities notified me that my services were no longer needed.

Not to teach! It seemed like a living death, but the Lord had plans for me that were better than I could have dreamed possible.

I had no sooner fallen in love with the Word than the Lord laid it on my heart to share it with others. The congregation that at first rejected me soon made me an officer and put me in charge of soul winning and outreach. Also, I became a Sabbath school teacher and youth leader and was involved in many other church departments and activities.

I was occupied in this way when a call came from the church leaders for me to become a Bible worker. What a joy! Now I would be teaching again, and this time it was to share the precious news of salvation with so many hungry souls.

A few months later I was invited to become an associate pastor in charge of a small congregation in a nearby community called Romelié. This was a shock. Who was I to be doing this work? If I were older, if I were married, if I were a man, if I had more experience, maybe I could do it. But when I took the matter to the Lord, He said to me, "Just use what you have, Gilma, and leave the results to Me."

As the months went by, I learned as never before to cling to the Lord. And I became convinced that the prophecies of Joel are being fulfilled, that His Spirit really is being poured out on handmaids and servants in these last days.

Of course, it was not easy. There were older men in the congregation who were not happy that the conference had sent a woman to be their spiritual leader. They said nothing to me directly, but their attitude made their feelings plain. As time went on, however, and they saw how the Lord was blessing, their hearts were softened, and one by one these noble men came and confessed their feelings and said that they now could see that God accepts women as well as men to labor in His cause, and we came to have a close relationship of confidence and mutual appreciation.

Soon news came that there was to be a coordinated national evangelistic campaign. About that time I suffered a badly sprained ankle with torn ligaments. This happened in October. The meetings were to start in November, and the Romelié company was to bring eight souls for the Lord. So I talked to the Lord about it. "What am I going to do, Lord? I can't even walk. There is no way I can get out and give Bible studies? How am I going to find eight souls for You?"

But He said to me, "Don't worry, Gilma. Not by might nor by power, but by My Spirit." When the meetings began, the Lord performed a miracle. Some folks who had attended only occasionally, and others who had never come before, began to attend. In spite of my being unable to prepare the groundwork and before the meetings were over, eight precious souls had surrendered to the Lord.

The months hurried by, and as my first year of service drew to a close, instead of 15 baptized members in Romelié, there were 35. Praise His holy name!

But this blessing was also a serious problem. The little congregation was meeting in someone's living room, and with so many members, plus all their children and visitors, we were desperately overcrowded. I spoke with the district pastor and told him we needed a new church building.

He smiled. "Of course you do, Gilma, but for now it's just a dream. We don't have any money for a project like that and neither does the conference."

He told me this on a Tuesday. On Friday night I went to bed fasting, and I prayed for many hours. On Sabbath morning there were visitors in church. Some folks were visiting Cuba from the United States, and somehow they found our little congregation all the way out on the eastern end of the island. Of course we welcomed them warmly. It was a hot day, and when these dear people saw so many folks crowding into that small space in the midst of the suffocating heat, they were moved.

Before they left, they handed me an envelope, saying, "Here, Gilma. Maybe you can use this to start a fund for a new building."

When we opened the envelope, we found $390 inside. We exchanged that money for 8,000 Cuban pesos. Our visitors did not know it, but in that part of the island that amount was more than enough to solve our problem.

We located a house with a large living room and began to pray that the authorities would allow us to buy it for a family of believers who would live there and allow us to use the space for our meetings.

I was busy with this project when another surprise came. The conference notified me that they had voted to send me to study at the Cuban Adventist Seminary located near Havana.

Once again I went to my best Friend, and said, "Lord, we're just starting this project. How can I leave it right now?"

But He said to me, "It's all right, Gilma. The idea was yours. Now another person will finish it. You continue to follow My plans for your life, and everything will turn out all right."

That is precisely what I plan to do, and I don't have the slightest doubt that He will keep His word.

Gilma Carbonell is now senior pastor of the Seventh-day Adventist Central Church in Guantánamo, Cuba.

Chapter 22

I Found the Superstar

. . . .

Reiko Matsumoto

When I was 16, I saw a film called *Jesus Christ Superstar*. I had heard of Jesus before, but I knew almost nothing about Him. The film was shocking to me. It created in my heart a fervent desire to know Jesus, and I eagerly went back to see the movie again and again.

When I left the theater that first time, a man was handing out tracts. The movie ended with the Crucifixion, but the tract said that Jesus' life did not end at the cross and that He was resurrected and is going to come again. The tract contained an invitation to enroll in a correspondence course to study the Bible. I started at once. As I studied, I was filled with happiness to learn that God is love. Knowing about Jesus changed me little by little. I discovered true love, which is completely different from the love of this world. More than anything, I wanted to be like Him.

There was, however, a serious problem: I loved Jesus and His teachings, but I couldn't understand the cross, and the correspondence lessons said that this was the most important point. I kept asking, *Why did He have to die for me?* I went to church once, but my father found out and forbade me to go again. I did not establish a church connection, so as time went on my heart strayed from the love I had felt at first. Finally I decided to go ahead and live a good life on my own without God.

I finished high school and enrolled in a university. Everything there was new and attractive. I was happy at first, but I continued to have a thirst for truth. So I took a philosophy class and read books about several religions. But none of that satisfied my heart, and I began to realize that I could not live without God. Just when I was starting to seek Him again, I received a postcard with an invitation to enroll in another Bible course. I sent in the card, but about that time I became interested in spiritualism. As a result, my heart was hardened against what the Bible course taught.

I had a friend whom I admired because she was sincere and very bright.

One day she invited me to attend a meeting of the Unification Church.* I had heard negative things about these people, so I rejected the invitation, but she insisted with tears. I was astonished because she was a calm and cool person. So I said, "Just once." It occurred to me that I might be able to rescue her from that eccentric cult.

I expected the Unification members to be weird people, but they were friendly and sincere, and I could see they were faithful. As I observed them, my prejudice fell away. I continued to attend and started to study their doctrines. The coordinator (pastor) taught me with great fervor and enthusiasm. He talked a lot about spirits in the invisible world. I was interested in spiritism at the time and so was very much attracted to this teaching. Their ardent sermons captured my heart. They quoted the Bible, so I didn't doubt they were telling the truth. I was thrilled especially because they said that the Unification Church would unite all religions, science, and everything. I began to share the enthusiasm and was convinced that this church was fantastic.

After I had been attending the Unification Church for some time, I had a disturbing experience. I woke up at midnight with a terrible weight pressing on my chest. It was impossible to get up or even to breathe. In terror I tried to cry out, but I found I couldn't do that, either. With great effort I opened my eyes.

When I did, the weight lifted, but I could see nothing in the darkness. After a while my nerves calmed down and I tried to get some more sleep, but as soon as I closed my eyes the crushing weight was back. This experience was repeated the next night and for several nights after that. Each time it left me feeling weaker and more exhausted. If I had doubted the existence of spirits and invisible forces in the world, it was impossible to do so after that.

I told the coordinator of our church what had happened. He smiled and said, "Don't worry. That means you are one of the chosen."

"But what should I do?" I asked him anxiously.

"You have to work harder," he replied. And that is what I tried to do. The coordinator said that God wanted me to save my dead ancestors and also other spirits who were placing their hopes on me. I had to do this by praying long hours and working very hard to achieve total purification of my being.

I dedicated myself completely to the activities of the church. In carrying out this principle, some of the other members even separated themselves from their families and lived together or with other members. If anyone had money or possessions, these too had to be turned over to the church without reservation.

When I was in my last year at the university, the coordinator spoke to me. "You must not finish," he said. "We want you to remain in the university so you can continue to evangelize and teach others our ways."

"But how can I do that?" I asked him, very perplexed. "I'm about to graduate."

"It's simple," he said cheerfully. "You must fail your classes so you can repeat the year."

I was horrified. One of the main rules of the church is obedience, and the word of the coordinator is received as the voice of God. But in our culture, failing even a single class brings shame, not only for the student, but for the entire family. Furthermore, my father had spent so much money on me. He had supported me with great effort and sacrifice during my college years. And now to tell him I would have to repeat the year—it was simply unthinkable! With great feelings of anguish and guilt I disobeyed the coordinator and graduated.

This, of course, was a very bad "sin," and I knew I would have to carry out a difficult and painful punishment because of what I had done. I started to get up early every day and pray for 40 minutes. The church had taught us that the number 40 is very important, so I was careful to keep this in mind. I also began fasting, sometimes for one day and others for three. I don't remember how many times I did this until I finally felt I had removed the guilt.

Not long after joining the Unification movement, I invited my sister, and she also embraced the faith. At her university the Unificationists were very active. Together with other young people, my sister visited many places under difficult conditions to preach the Word. It was summer, and the weather was very hot, but there were no showers, and they didn't have much food. These were young people from good families, but they had to beg for money to pay their expenses. They told people they were collecting money for the poor in other countries. That was a lie, but the leaders explained that it is all right to lie for God.

Several times my sister called me crying and saying, "Reiko, this is very hard." I tried to encourage her, but I knew she was telling the truth, because I was involved in similar activities.

After my graduation I began to teach Japanese calligraphy in two high schools. I greatly enjoyed working with the young people, but I felt guilty because I was not dedicating myself to the church full-time. So, as compensation, I gave them my entire salary.

The Unification Church teaches that the second coming of Christ has already taken place in the person of Mr. Moon and that he is completing and perfecting the work that Jesus began. I had a photograph of our leader in my room, and every morning and every evening I worshipped before it.

The friend who invited me to the Unification Church also led another friend to join. That girl became faithful and fervent in the faith. When her father forbade her to go anymore, she ran away from home and stayed at the church. Her father came and took her back. He locked her in the house and hid her shoes, but she escaped and ran back to the church barefoot. This happened more than once, until her father became very angry. "Your church is harmful to you and to society," he shouted. "I'm your father and am responsible for this affair, so I am going to kill you and then myself." He raised a knife and lunged at her, but her mother intervened, crying hysterically, and thus saved the life of her only daughter. But the mother got sick as a result.

One day not long after this, this mother heard about Pastor Waga, a Seventh-day Adventist minister who was helping young people who were involved in the Unification movement. She and her husband asked the pastor to come and speak with their daughter. Tenderly he explained the differences between the teachings of the Unification Church and the Bible. As soon as her eyes were opened, this girl communicated what she had learned to the friend who had invited me. My friend, too, met with Pastor Waga, and she felt a responsibility to tell me about what she had learned.

One summer day I received a phone call from my friend, and she said she wanted me to meet someone. I went to her house, and there was Pastor Waga. After exchanging greetings and engaging in a few words of friendly conversation, he said, "I understand you are a member of the Unification Church; is that right?"

"Yes," I answered.

"Do you believe this church teaches the truth?"

"Yes, of course."

Then he said, "Can you tell me what your church teaches?"

I knew a lot about what I had experienced, but I found it difficult to give a brief answer about the beliefs. Anyway, I told him a few things.

Then he said, "Can you tell me what is the support for those points?"

This direct and simple question came as a complete surprise to me. I quickly reviewed in my mind the things that had brought me to surrender my heart and life so fully to that church. First of all, I was impressed by the fervor and devotion of the members. I also appreciated the veneration and respect they had for their ancestors. Furthermore, I saw it as a religion of hope because it teaches that all religions and all nations will unite under the leadership of Mr. Moon. For those and other reasons, I had believed. But at that moment I realized that all my reasons were subjective. I had no real or solid basis for my faith.

The pastor saw that I was upset and confused by his question, so he began speaking to me in a kind way, and I soon realized he knew more about Unification beliefs than I did. He gave me a complete summary of what the church teaches.

Then he mentioned a Bible passage the group frequently uses. I knew that what he said was true because I had often heard this verse. Next he opened his Bible and read the complete passage in its context. I suddenly realized that the true meaning of the verse was not what they said it meant. Their teaching was based on only a partial quotation. In this way he continued to open the Scripture and show me point after point how Unification teachings are based on a partial and selective use of the Bible texts.

I understood then that what I had believed so passionately was false. It was a devastating experience. I didn't want to accept what the pastor was saying, but it was impossible to deny. At that moment everything I had held dear came crashing to the ground. I didn't know what to do. I felt shattered. I could believe nothing, nobody. I fell into a deep depression that lasted for several months. During that time I wanted to take my life but didn't have the courage. I wanted to go crazy to escape my thoughts. I wandered aimlessly and without hope. My heart was empty.

Then one day I received an invitation to attend the Adventist church. I think they were wise to leave me alone for a while, because I didn't want to talk to anyone at first. But at that time Pastor Waga asked Pastor Matsuzaka to get in touch with me. He called me and led me little by little with tenderness, and he recommended that I take the "Voice of Prophecy" Bible course. I did so, and God's words began to fill my emptiness. Slowly, peace came back to my heart.

I began attending the Adventist church. I liked it very much, but I soon came up against the same stumbling block as before: I still could not understand the cross.

One day they invited me to attend a Communion service. I said no because I was not a church member, and I thought it was a solemn ceremony. But the pastor and other members said, "You can watch, at least." So I went.

I learned that washing feet was the humblest work in Jesus' time. It impressed me powerfully that Jesus, the King of kings, the Lord of lords, the Ruler of the universe, washed His disciples' feet. As I saw how the members illustrated this wonderful act, the great reality struck home, and I was overwhelmed.

Then the pastor read from the Bible: "Take, eat, this is my body. It was broken for you." Then I could see that Jesus' love and sacrifice went far beyond washing His disciples' feet.

This thought impacted me in a powerful way. What had been so dark and confusing was now clear. What an incredible sacrifice! What amazing love! And it was for me! That is the meaning of the cross. As these revelations became crystal clear, I wept.

I wanted to wipe my experience with the Unification Church from my memory. I hated it, but God had permitted it for my sake. Having passed through that experience, I could now better comprehend the depths of His love, and without hesitation I joyfully accepted Jesus and His great sacrifice on my behalf. Soon after that I was baptized, and now I rejoice every day in His wonderful love.

After her baptism, Reiko taught Japanese calligraphy at San-iku Junior High School, a Seventh-day Adventist institution. She later married Seiji Masumoto, a physician. They have two children, Yukiko and Naoki.

---

* This is the group that is sometimes called "Moonies" because the founder is Sun Myung Moon.

Chapter 23

I Don't Need Those Things Anymore

. . . .

Larry Lichtenwalter

When Debbie came to our church for the first time, she was elegantly dressed. She wore a white mink coat and extravagant jewelry and cosmetics. She had achieved spectacular success as a real estate professional, and now she was living to the height of her new wealth. In her parties she offered her guests a little silver platter with pure cocaine and rolled-up $100 bills to aspirate it. She drove the latest in luxury vehicles and lived in a gorgeous mansion. She seemed to have it all, but in reality she was lacking what was most essential, and now she had come, hoping to find it with us.

At first I wondered how she would fit in with our people, but I needn't have worried. From the start, it was clear that she enjoyed the experience immensely. The members of our congregation are warm and friendly, and they open their hearts to visitors and make them feel at home. Debbie responded with enthusiasm and soon became an integral part of the life of the church. She clearly enjoyed the Christian friendships she made as she worshipped God with us. No one ever mentioned her lifestyle or the way she dressed.

I will never forget the day when Debbie told me she wanted to be baptized. *Whoa!* I thought. *Why are you talking to me about baptism when your lifestyle hasn't changed?*

That's what I thought; what I really said was "Of course, Debbie! When would you like to do it?"

"Next Sabbath," she responded enthusiastically.

"Ah, . . . well, yes. That's wonderful," I said. "When can we sit down and talk about a few things?"

The only time she had available was one hour before Sabbath school on the day of her baptism. I wasn't too worried, because she had accepted without hesitation everything we had studied together in the Bible. With regard to certain matters such as personal adornment and Christian lifestyle, I prefer to allow the Holy Spirit to lead in His own way and time. That is why I hadn't wanted to have this conversation earlier.

What a beautiful surprise that Sabbath morning when I met with Debbie to talk about her baptism. She was beautiful, attractively dressed, with exquisite taste—as always—but with no jewelry or makeup of any kind. She looked stunningly beautiful, but very, very different. I was tempted to say something, but I held my peace. When the right time came during our conversation, I asked her what she thought about Christian dress and adornment.

"Pastor," she said, "I don't need those things anymore. What I need is right there . . . in the water." She was pointing to the baptismal tank.

The apostle Paul apparently had this same idea, because he wrote, "I also want the women to dress modestly, with decency and propriety, adorning themselves, not with elaborate hairstyles or gold or pearls or expensive clothes, but with good deeds, appropriate for women who profess to worship God" (1 Tim. 2:9, 10, NIV). And Peter adds, "Your beauty should not come from outward adornment, such as elaborate hairstyles and the wearing of gold jewelry or fine clothes. Rather, it should be that of your inner self, the unfading beauty of a gentle and quiet spirit, which is of great worth in God's sight" (1 Peter 3:3, 4, NIV).

That's how it is when love for God has first place in our hearts. The tangible expressions of culture that compete with Christian values no longer occupy center stage. They become less and less important, until they disappear—whether we're talking about matters of music, entertainment, what we read or watch, how we dress, or whatever. These things, which formerly dominated our lives, lose their power. When our relationship with Christ is a beautiful reality, when we love God above all things and spend time with Him in His Word, our hearts will be filled with delight in what He has given us. Then we will come to understand the insignificance of these material things.

As Debbie said: "Pastor, I don't need those things anymore."

Chapter 24

Dear Tony

Jackie Flynt Payne

Dear Tony, I can't believe it's been a year since you first knocked on my door and invited Bob and me to a Bible study. How our lives have changed in just 12 months! A few weeks ago, as I was welcoming folks to Sabbath school, I remembered our first visitors' dinner with you and Mary. You said to your wife, "Mary, can't you just see Jackie as a Sabbath school superintendent?" I didn't even know what a Sabbath school superintendent was; now I am one.

I think I was born to be a Seventh-day Adventist. You've probably read the poem "Footprints," which speaks of seeing Christ's footprints along the path of one's life. I can clearly see Christ's footprints bringing me first to Him and then to fellowship in His remnant church.

I grew up in a devout Southern Baptist home in a small, conservative Southern Baptist community in central Mississippi. I accepted Christ and was baptized when I was 8 years old. My daddy was a deacon, and we were at church every time the doors were open. The only Adventist I knew was a woman who upholstered furniture in our town. I remember riding my bike past her house on a Saturday morning, wondering what people who went to church on Saturday looked like. Did they wear Sunday clothes to church on Saturday?

As an adult I taught Sunday school and Vacation Bible School. I wrote denominational articles and curriculum materials for children's discipleship and missions for the Southern Baptist Convention. I was the pastor's secretary at a large Baptist church. I had no reason to believe I would ever be anything but a Southern Baptist until the day I died, at which point I planned on joining my Baptist ancestors in heaven.

And then (all the stories about God's work seem to have an "and then…") around the beginning of 1998 I was reading a book by Zig Ziglar called *Top Performance*. The chapter titled "Education to Overcome Management Paralysis" challenged me. Ziglar wrote about our fears: "If you have the courage to write them down, here is what you will find: Out of the ten items you listed, seven or eight will already have happened or cannot happen. Of the remaining items, you have absolutely no control over one or two of them. And you will find that only one or two items are within your control."

I made my list, and it went something like this: fear of getting cancer, fear of getting heart disease, fear of losing my job, fear of not being able to work, fear of not being able to pay my bills, etc. As I studied my list, I began to realize one common element: my health was directly or indirectly related to all of those fears over which I had some control. Managing those fears depended upon one thing: being healthy. And it made more sense to me to stay healthy than to overcome an illness and return to health.

I knew that the source of health and wisdom is God. I knew that my body is God's temple. But it never occurred to me that my lackadaisical attitude toward health issues—my terrible eating habits, my aversion to exercise—was a spiritual problem. I knew that God would direct me to the truth and health, so I began an intensive study of the Bible. Simultaneously I began researching solid health principles on the Internet.

My study focused on four principles: eat right, exercise religiously, rest routinely, and relax regularly (this was nine months before I ever heard the Adventist health message).

During Bible study one day, I read this verse from 3 John 2: "Beloved, I pray that you may prosper in all things and be in health, just as your soul prospers" (NKJV). I understood the part about being in health and prospering, But what, I wondered, did John mean when he wrote about soul prosperity, and how could I achieve it?

This became my battle cry each day: "God, give me soul prosperity. Show me how to prosper my soul."

God began leading me through a study of the Old Testament, emphasizing scriptural references to obedience and keeping His commandments, including the Sabbath. In my prayer journal I wrote, "How do I keep the Sabbath, God? Show me. I go to church every Sunday."

About this time I went to the mailroom at work and saw a little magazine called *Happiness Digest* lying on the counter. I picked it up and examined it. I read the index of articles and felt that it would be helpful in my quest for soul purity. I took it home and read it carefully. I found that everything in that magazine agreed perfectly with what I believed. The next day I carefully returned the magazine to the mailroom.

There was a card inside the magazine that offered Bible studies on other topics, so I selected a topic that I thought would be beneficial and mailed the card to the obscure address in Maryland. I received the Bible study, found it helpful, and didn't think any more about it.

As summer came, I continued my search for soul prosperity. In August I began to hear talk about Y2K, and I mentioned it to my husband, Bob. We discussed the Bible prophecies concerning the end of the age. We turned to Matthew 24 but stopped when we got to verse 20: "Pray that your flight will not take place in winter or on the Sabbath" (NIV).

"That's strange," I said to Bob, "January 1, 2000, will be in the winter. I wonder if it will be on the Sabbath." So we got out a calendar and were relieved to find that the beginning of Y2K would be on Saturday, not Sunday. "But," I reminded him, "in Jesus' day Saturday was the Sabbath."

Bob didn't believe me, so we looked up all the verses we could find on the Sabbath. We discovered that Sabbath is indeed the seventh day of the week.

About this time I had begun to feel a sense of restlessness of spirit. I felt homesick, and I didn't know what I was homesick for. Bob and I were members of a large Baptist church. It was the kind of church that you could miss going to for a month of Sundays and no one would know you were absent. We thought that maybe God was leading us to find a smaller church.

We began visiting another Baptist church in our area. We liked the music and the preaching, and one Sunday night we decided to become members. In all my years of being a Baptist, I had never been to a church service on Sunday night when an invitation to join the church was not extended. But that night no invitation was given. Bob and I were stunned. We continued to attend that church, but we decided not to join it.

One evening in September 1998 you came to our front door. That my husband let you, a stranger, into our home was a miracle. That God pried my hands from my ears and my heart long enough to listen to you was the greatest miracle of all.

I couldn't understand how you had my card, mailed months before, and why you were doing a follow-up to see if I had received the materials I had requested from *Happiness Digest*.

I was furious. "How did you get my card?" I demanded. "Did you come here all the way from Maryland?" You assured me that you lived in Panama City and that you were simply inviting Bob and me to a Bible study. Despite my questioning, you wouldn't tell me the name of your church. You denied that you were a Mormon or a Jehovah's Witness, but beyond that you wouldn't mention your denomination.

That infuriated me further. I quizzed you at length on every topic I could imagine, trying to cleverly trip you up: Who do you say Jesus is? How can a person be saved? And the one I was sure would get you: What do you believe about the Trinity? Nothing worked. I agreed with every answer you gave.

Still, I wasn't remotely interested in attending your Bible study. I coolly thanked you and, trying to get you out the door, agreed to accept the little book *Steps to Christ*.

When you left, I glanced through the book. I looked for a way to discover what denomination you represented.

The next morning I logged on to the Internet and typed in the words "Ellen White." I was totally dumbfounded when the search engine returned with scores of finds, all yielding the words "Seventh-day Adventist." I pored over the materials, intrigued by my findings. I took notes, wrote down questions.

I knew that a Seventh-day Adventist church was located several blocks from my office, so I called the church. A young man answered. My first question was "Is a man named Tony Brown a member of your church?"

"Yes," the man replied, "Tony is an elder of our church." Second, I wanted answers to some questions I had about the Bible. The young man passed the phone to the pastor.

Pastor Scott Tyman graciously offered to answer all my questions in person, rather than by phone. He said he would drop by on Thursday, two days away. I spent those two days reading everything I could about Seventh-day Adventists.

On Thursday Pastor Tyman answered all my questions but one. He had a little booklet about jewelry that he offered to me but then took it back. He'd hold it out and take it back. "It might be too much too soon," he said.

I took the book and began reading it the minute Pastor Tyman left. As I read, I knew I was reading the truth. I began removing my earrings and necklace even before I finished.

I felt like someone who had been starved for years and was finally being offered a great banquet. My soul just seemed to soak up all the Bible's teachings. All the questions I'd had for so many years were finally answered—the Baptist theology that didn't make sense (under grace, not under law), the issues that ministers had skirted around (why Baptists keep nine of the 10 commandments), the conflicted teachings (the dead in Christ will rise first)—and were suddenly clear to me.

The very next Sabbath Bob and I attended the Panama City Seventh-day

Adventist Church. We felt we had come home. In God's timing we came to the church just as NET '98 was about to begin. God graciously provided this intensive learning opportunity to introduce us to Adventist teachings. Bob and I were baptized in November, two months after we met you.

And then just a few short months later you, Mary, and your daughter, Megan, moved to Mississippi.

You moved while we were in the midst of an Amazing Facts seminar. What a change that brought to our church. Space problems are the best kind to have in a church, don't you think? We've had almost 80 new members join the church!

While we wrestle with sanctuary seating, parking, and Sabbath school classroom space, I also worry about the new members. When Bob and I were new to the church, we had so many wonderful friends who took us under their wings—you and Mary, the Schwinns, the Lugos, the Coves—to teach us, to fellowship with us, to go camping with us, and to answer our endless questions, such as "What do you do on Sabbath?" I hope all these new family members will find mentors and friends who will include them, guide them, and lovingly instruct them as our friends did for us. Does it take a village to raise a new Adventist?

I've saved the best for last. Our daughter Leslie is now a senior in high school. At first Leslie was certain that Bob and I had gotten mixed up with a cult. ("After all, Mother, people who are in a cult don't know it.") But we, and many others, prayed for Leslie. She started reading materials we brought home. This spring she did a term paper on the "Saturday-Sunday shuffle." And this summer Leslie told Pastor Scott she wanted to be baptized.

A few weeks ago when she stood before the congregation to read the scripture, Leslie said, "Good morning, church family. Happy Sabbath!"

All I could say was "Praise God!"

I'm not homesick anymore. We love our new church family, and we're so grateful for the opportunities that God has given us to serve Him and His church. I thank Him for lovingly uniting our whole family in such a wonderful church home.

God promises, "You will know the truth, and the truth will set you free" (John 8:32, NIV). God showed me the truth, and it has changed my life forever. And it all began because you were faithful to knock on one door. I can never thank you enough for your persistence and your patience.

Your sister in Christ.

Chapter 25

A Message for Me

. . . .

Leroy Moore

As a young pastor in Fairbanks, Alaska, I used to start my sermon preparation on Sunday morning. Then, during the whole week, I would dedicate two or three hours every morning to the task. One year the time was approaching for our annual Ingathering campaign in which our members contact their friends and neighbors and invite them to contribute to the outreach activities of the church. Because of the importance of this message, I decided to begin its preparation two or three months in advance. But instead of being able to relax the week before the message was to be presented as I expected would be the case, I had to dedicate more time to it than usual. In fact, I never was able to prepare that sermon.

The Sunday before the Sabbath on which I was to give the message I sat down to go over the outline I had already prepared, and I discovered it was dead in the water. No matter how hard I tried, I could do nothing to revive it, so I decided to prepare a different sermon altogether. But every time I thought I had a message from the Lord, it, too, died in my hands. As the days passed, my perplexity increased. This was indeed a strange experience. Never before had the Holy Spirit failed to guide me in choosing and preparing a sermon.

By Friday I was getting desperate. But as I meditated on the problem that afternoon, I suddenly understood that I should do nothing more. The Lord wanted to give me a message. That night I shared what was happening with one of the church school teachers and invited her to pray with me. We were still on our knees when the passage of Isaiah 60:1-3 came vividly into my thoughts.

I arose and informed her that I knew what my text was to be. I then went to bed early and did not get up until 7:30 a.m. I did not read the passage until a few minutes before leaving for church, and even then I avoided formulating ideas as to what I was going to say. This was clearly a Holy Spirit-led message.

As I sat on the platform that morning, an unknown woman came in with a little girl. Naturally, I wondered who she might be. Was she visiting in the area? Or was she a new Adventist who had just arrived in the city?

Or could she be a non-Adventist? I was still pondering this when the hymn ended and it was time for me to read my text.

"Arise, shine; for your light has come, and the glory of the Lord has risen upon you. For behold, darkness will cover the earth, and deep darkness the peoples; but the Lord will rise upon you, and His glory will appear upon you. And nations will come to your light, and kings to the brightness of your rising" (Isa. 60:1-3, NASB).

The Lord gave me words to explain that passage with greater clarity than if I had carefully prepared. The glory of the Lord is His character that He wants to reveal through us as He rises upon us like the dawn. I explained that this is related to the loud cry of the angel of Revelation 18, whose glory is to fill the whole earth. The visitor listened carefully as I explained how the nations who do not know the message, and even their civil authorities, will come to that light.

I had never related that passage to Ingathering and was familiar with only verses 1-3, but near the close of the sermon I was directed to read also the verses that follow and apply them to God's purpose, that we, through the Ingathering program, can claim the treasures of God that are in the hands of the world.

Referring to Revelation 17:15, I explained that the passage "The abundance of the sea shall be converted unto thee" (Isa. 60:5) means that in the last days people from many nations will respond to the judgment-hour message, and when it says "the wealth of the nations will come to you," it refers to God's purpose that the riches that are in the hands of the world will be brought into His treasury to be used in the proclamation of the three angels' messages.

At the door of the church the visitor exclaimed with great enthusiasm, "God gave you that message just for me!" But she refused to give me any other information except her name, Pat Wilmouth.

Feeling that the Lord had truly given me that message for her, I invited her to our home for lunch. She said that she could not accept, but it seemed to me she really wanted to. So I persisted with the invitation. When she said she had to go because her husband was waiting for her at home, I said, "Go and bring him." She assured me that he would never accept such an invitation. But because I saw in her eyes the desire to accept, I told her we would wait until 2:30 p.m. to see if she could persuade him.

At 3:00 my wife and I finally sat down to eat. But just as we were bowing our heads to thank God for the food, the doorbell rang. I opened the door, and there was Pat, and behind her was an enormous man whom she introduced as her husband, Bud. When we were seated at the table, I asked about his background, and he told us he was a former Adventist.

Bud told us that he was studying in an evangelical college in preparation for the ministry when he accepted the Adventist message and transferred to Atlantic Union College. While there he had become bitter. He left the college and moved to Alaska, hoping to distance himself entirely and permanently from Adventism.

That Sabbath morning, two years later, their little girl, who was then 4 years old, began to beg Pat to take her to Sabbath school. That was exceedingly strange. She had not gone to Sabbath school for two years and had not even heard the words mentioned since she was 2 years old.

Pat said no, but her little girl would not accept that answer, and she kept on begging. Again and again she said, "Please, Mommy, take me to Sabbath school." Sabbath school was over when Pat finally yielded to her insistence and brought her to our church, which is only two miles from their house.

After Bud finished telling me this story, I invited him to surrender to Christ and come back to church. I did not know that that same morning he had made his wife take an oath: "Under no circumstances are you to tell the pastor where we live." She had obeyed, but now the Holy Spirit was working on Bud's heart.

He asked me if we could talk privately. When we were alone in my office, he told me he had never prayed, not even when he was studying for the ministry. In all my experience, seldom have I seen the struggle between the forces of good and evil as clearly as I did that day. Perspiration rolled off his distorted face as he tried again and again to say yes, but he could only repeat, "I can't." I struggled with him and for him for three hours. He continued to say he wanted to surrender but could not. At last, with tears, he poured out his soul before God in prayer.

After that, Bud and Pat were in church every Sabbath. And they enthusiastically took part in the Ingathering campaign, which had before been an especially objectionable point to them, but interestingly enough was what had most touched Pat's heart that morning as she listened to my "impromptu" sermon.

What began with a little girl asking to go to Sabbath school ended with a family giving their hearts to God. That was the beginning to a new life of peace and a close relationship with God for both Bud and Pat. When I met them many years later, I was delighted to find that they continued to be faithful, joyous Christians. As leaders in their church, they were involved with heart and soul in its activities—including the annual Ingathering program!

Chapter 26

When God Used Kevin

. . . .

Barry Gane

K evin came to one of my evangelistic meetings in England. In it two people surrendered their lives to the Lord—not thousands, just two. And one of them was Kevin.

And how he began! He arrived early for every meeting. He encouraged others by his fervor. When it was his turn to pray or sing or anything else, he did it with all his heart.

"You have to realize the change that has come into my life," he told me. "How could I not be happy and thankful to God?"

But time goes on, and life continues. One day I saw Kevin come in after the meeting had already started. He sat at the back with his hands in his pockets.

I said to him, "Kevin, in the Christian life there is a paradox. What we keep, we lose; and what we give away, we keep."

"That sounds like a riddle," he said.

"Yes, but there's nothing complicated about it. If you keep Jesus, if you hold Him as a secret and don't let anybody else know about Him, very soon you will lose Him. But if you share Him, telling other people what He has done in your life, not only will you keep the joy alive, but also it will grow."

"So what do you say we go to the park and witness?" responded Kevin. I think he was testing me to find out if I really believed what I said.

"Let's do it!" I answered.

We organized a group of young people, and that afternoon we went downtown to the city center. We congregated on the steps of the city hall, and soon a large crowd of people came over to hear what we had to say. Some rockers with blue, green, purple hair; shaved heads; and pierced ears, cheeks, noses, eyebrows, and belly buttons came over and sat on the steps behind us to harass us.

I started to speak, and they began to make fun of us. They shouted hysterically, "Oh, yes, preach it, brother! Hallelujah! Amen!" . . . things like that. They really gave me a rough time. After a while I stopped and got down off the box I was standing on as a makeshift platform. Then the young people from the church began to play their guitars and sing.

At that point Kevin came over and said, "Pastor, it's my turn now; I want to speak."

"You don't have to do it, Kevin," I said. "God loves you anyway."

He looked at me surprised, but I insisted, "Not today, Kevin. You can speak some other time."

I said this because I didn't want him to get discouraged because of how hard it was. But he insisted. "I want to speak today."

We went a little way from where they were all shouting and mocking, and I prayed for Kevin. At six and a half feet tall and as thin as a broomstick, his whole body shook violently.

Lord, take away his nervousness, I prayed.

In my mind I was praying that the Lord would keep him alive so he would not die of nerves in front of all these people. Do you know why I was praying like that? Because that had been my problem for a long time, and I could understand perfectly how he felt.

Then Kevin prayed, "Dear Lord, thank You for all You have done for me. Please speak through me today. I want them to see Jesus. Amen."

When we went back to where the people were, the music stopped. Kevin did not need to stand on any box to be seen, so he simply began to speak. When he did, the people stopped shouting and came up close because he was speaking softly since his voice was trembling so much. After a few introductory words, he turned his back on the crowd, looked directly at the rockers on the steps, and said to them, "Hello, guys. You know me. I'm Kevin."

At that they all began to shout, "It's him! It really is! It's Kevin!"

They all knew him! I didn't realize it, but these were his old friends. Then in a quiet voice he began to share an extremely simple message. He talked to them about Jesus and His love. His words broke through the barrier and reached them in a way I never could have.

Before long all these young people had come down from the steps and were gathered around. They asked him hundreds of questions. They wanted to know what had happened, what was going on in his life. And simply and clearly, Kevin shared Jesus with them.

At the end, it occurred to him to do something unthinkable. He invited them all to church!

I'm not sure if my church members are ready for this, I thought. *What will happen when all these rockers come in dressed the way they are?*

From the park we went directly to the youth meeting at our church, and a large number of people from the park came with us.

When we entered the church, the first person who jumped out of her seat to welcome them was a 75-year-old woman with white hair. She hugged every one of those kids.

A miracle occurred that day . . . well, actually, more than one, because Kevin's faith began to blaze again; and furthermore, the Lord had used him powerfully to reach a group of young people who urgently needed to hear the message of God's love for them.

Chapter 27

I Can Believe Again!

. . . .

Elaine Kennedy

At 7 years old I was lying in my dark bedroom saying a prayer to God, when I realized that my words were bouncing off the ceiling and hitting me in the face. God was not with me in my heart, but out there somewhere—and there was a great blackness between us. I couldn't reach Him, and I knew, truly knew, that it was my fault. Terror leaked from my heart into every bone of my body, and suddenly I had to run to the safety of my parents' presence in the living room. I dropped to the floor and hugged my mother's knees. Looking up into her face, I cried, "Oh, Mama! Something terrible is happening! I have been praying to God, but He won't hear me, and it's all my fault."

Daddy jumped up off of the couch and turned off the TV. That shocked me. I turned to him and begged, "Please, you've got to pray for me!"

At that moment my father uttered words that I didn't think parents were allowed to say to their children. "I can't pray for you, Elaine." I turned toward my mother, and he said, "Your mother can't pray for you either."

Mama intervened with the tenderest name she had for me. "Oh, Laney, the Holy Spirit is calling you to repentance."

My heart pounded as Daddy continued: "Your mother and I cannot be saved *for* you. Only you can pray the prayer that is needed now. Go back to your room and pray."

At that moment I panicked. "But what am I supposed to say? I don't know what to say!"

The answer was simple: "Tell God what's in your heart."

In anguish I returned to my bed and poured out my heart. "Oh, God, I hate this feeling, and I know it's my fault. Please, God, please forgive me. I don't ever want to feel like this again." A warm peace filled me, and I fell asleep. And from that early age God was an important part of my life.

We were Southern Baptists and held conservative religious beliefs that included a Creator and a recent creation. These beliefs were not challenged until my ninth-grade biology class, when I had to write a report on the book *On the Origin of Species,* by Charles Darwin. What I read must have made me quite furious, because my teacher wrote on my paper, "Elaine, don't let one man's ideas upset you so much."

During that same ninth-grade year another change that would have a profound effect on my belief system occurred: a new pastor was hired at my church. His first sermon was on Creation, and he began by telling us that we had misunderstood Genesis. I was startled. He didn't say our interpretation of the text was wrong, but rather that we had not fully understood its meaning. He then proceeded to introduce us to theistic evolution.

I was thrilled. I could merge my science and my Bible. During that one sermon I fully embraced the concept and gave up my Creator for a "Divine Guide" in the long process of evolution. The theological implications of such a transition are profound, but 14-year-old girls don't know very much about theology, and I quickly became a diehard theistic evolutionist.

This change in my theology did not result in a slipping and sliding away from God; my commitment to Him was as strong as ever. When I turned 16, my father gave me a car, and with that my church attendance increased. God was very close to me during those years even as my understanding of who He is became more confused.

When the time came to enroll in college, I had no problem selecting a major; as a science lover, I would study history. It doesn't sound logical now, but at the time it seemed to be the right thing to do.

Things, however, did not go quite as I had planned. In the second semester I enrolled in a class called Geology Concepts for Teachers. It was spectacular, and by midsemester I had changed my major to geology.

The following year I took my first class on fossils—invertebrate paleontology—the study of animals without a backbone that have been preserved in rocks. The course was fascinating and included field trips. There was one trip I will never forget. We crawled up the side of a hill noting the corals, snails, and clams buried in the dirt. I was the first to reach the top, so I sat down to enjoy the view. As I raised my left hand, I noticed something clinging to my palm, and I looked to see what it was. The tiny rocks, the size and shape of a kernel of wheat, were actually foraminifera, extinct one-celled marine animals. I looked down and realized that the "sand" I was sitting on consisted of countless millions of these creatures. I put my hands down into those forams and lifted them up, letting them run through my fingers like sand.

Suddenly I was stunned by the thought that these animals, billions of them, had lived and died before humans even existed. The Bible says that death came into the world because of sin. But theistic evolution, which was my view, meant that God had planned death, that He had used it to make evolution happen through the survival of the fittest. My heart exploded with emotion. *What kind of God do I serve? Would He deliberately create things to die? Did He actually bring about life as we know it today, and even human beings, through this bloody process? No! No! This is not my God! My God loves me!*

I cried . . . and no one asked me why. Again and again I asked the question, but no answers came. So finally I shelved it all. I refused to think about these issues anymore. I continued my studies, and I continued to be fervent and active in my church.

That didn't change until about a year after my honeymoon. I married a wonderful young man and dropped out of school. Dee and I had met at church, and during our first year of marriage we began attending a Bible study that was examining the book *The Late Great Planet Earth*, by Hal Lindsey. We were excited! Jesus was coming soon!

We were intensely interested in prophecy and end-time events, and it was around that time that the local paper carried an advertisement for a prophecy seminar with Adventist evangelist Kenneth Cox. On opening night we were there.

The meetings were riveting, and the sermon outlines that were provided for the attendees contained all the Bible texts that were used each evening. We could hardly wait to get home after each meeting. We would compare the texts with our book. The next evening we would go to the question-and-answer session after the service, and I would begin, "Hal Lindsey says," and Pastor Cox would respond, "Let's see what the Bible has to say about that."

As we continued to study, the entire Bible made sense for the first time in our lives. The messages were life-giving food for the soul, and we were ecstatic about the things we were learning until Pastor Cox preached the sermon "Adam's Mother's Birthday." In that message he talked about how God created the world in six days and rested on the seventh.

There were no questions from me that night. I marched down to the front and said to Pastor Cox: "You're crazy! You don't even know what you're talking about! I'm a geologist, and life on this earth is at least 600 million years old!"

The pastor didn't argue. He had only one question: "Will you come back tomorrow night? I have a book I'd like you to read. It's yours if you'll just come." I had no intention of returning, but hey, it was a free book; plus, we were happy with what we had learned in the previous meetings, so we went back and accepted the book. It was *Creation: Accident or Design?* by Harold Coffin.

I quickly discovered that Coffin did not write from a basis of ignorance. He wrote about the same rocks I had been studying for three years. He presented the same data. But he pointed to a radically different interpretation. I was up all night reading the book. By morning I understood that the facts are not the problem; the problem is the interpretation I had blindly accepted without realizing how much it had been determined by an underlying philosophy called naturalism. This philosophy teaches that absolutely the only thing that exists is the physical world. If you can't see it, measure it, or somehow detect it and explain it by natural law, it doesn't exist, and it never happened. It is a philosophical bias that underlies the interpretation of all natural phenomena in science today.

Joyfully I could see that the believer does not need to ignore or overlook any scientific fact. Nature, the world around us, can be understood in a way that is consistent with a conservative reading of Scripture. One contented thought dominated my mind: "I can believe the Bible again!"

In my work as a scientist today, I read journals and talk with people who remind me that what I believe is not the norm within the scientific community. At times I have encountered serious scientific arguments and reasoning that have challenged my faith. But by stripping away the rhetoric, explanations, and interpretations, the raw data is revealed, and in most cases, the information is consistent with a biblical understanding of earth history.

I admit that there are some things for which I do not have answers. These things do not destroy my faith but rather provide me with stimulating topics for prayer, thought, and research, because my faith is not based on scientific data. My faith is based on a living, intimate experience with God and His Word.

It is His gift.

———

Elaine Kennedy has a Ph.D. in geology from the University of Southern California. A consulting geologist, she is the author of Dinosaurs: Where Did They Come From . . . And Where Did They Go? *(Boise, Idaho: Pacific Press Pub. Assn., 2006).*

Sources

"A Gift From the River": original account by Doneshor Tripura.

"A Good Conversation": original account by Mario Veloso.

"One in a Million": Donald Berry. *Out of the Depths*. Boise, Idaho: Pacific Press Pub. Assn., 1989.

"A Lost Cause": Pat Grant. *Adventist Review*, Sept. 16, 1999.

"Unlikely Lamb": original account by Marco Huaco.

"Two Cents and Half a Cabbage": original account by Leslie Kay.

"Never Alone": original account by Álvaro Martínez-Jaimez.

"The Meaning of Life": original account by Ala and Elena Shuedova.

"The Change From Ten Centavos": Grace Hackett Lake. *Modern Mission Miracles*. Independent Publication, 1993.

"Aren't You Afraid?": Jevana Ben Maseko. *Adventist Review*, June 17, 2010.

"Do You Think There Is No Way Out?": original account by Carmen Hernández.

"Even a Mule": original account by Virgilio Zaldívar.

"Beloved Enemy": Jiri Drejnar. *Adventist Review*, Aug. 10, 2000.

"Leave Those Silly Fables!": Nicolás Chaij. *Milagros en mi vida*. Miami: Inter-American Division Pub. Assn., 1998.

"A Bus to Nowhere": adapted from Nicolás Chaij. *Milagros en mi vida*. Miami: Inter-American Division Pub. Assn., 1998.

"An Unchained Bible": original account by Ana Rodríguez de Gonzáles.

"Paths to Far Places": Ruth Wheeler. *Light the Paper Lantern*. Mountain View, Calif.: Pacific Press Pub. Assn., 1967.

"A Floor to Kneel On": John Baerg. *Brazil: Where the Action Is*. Privately published, 1973.

"Sometimes Change Is Like an Earthquake": Alcyon Fleck. *A Brand From the Burning*. Mountain View, Calif.: Pacific Press Pub. Assn., 1960.

"Korean Caveman": Theodora Wagnerin. *Dream Dragon's Escape*. Nashville: Southern Pub. Assn., 1968.

"God of the Unexpected": original account by Gilma Carbonell.

"I Found the Superstar": original account by Reiko Matsumoto.

"I Don't Need Those Things Anymore": original account by Larry Lichtenwalter.

"Dear Tony": Jackie Flynt Payne. *Review and Herald,* Nov. 23, 2000.

"A Message for Me": original account by Leroy Moore.

"When God Used Kevin": original account by Barry Gane.

"I Can Believe Again!": Elaine Kennedy. "How I Became a Creationist." *Signs of the Times,* September 2005.